ABOUT THE ROYAL SHAKESPEAI

The Royal Shakespeare Company at Stratl
formed in 1960 and gained its Royal Chart. ... .961. This year we
celebrate 50 years as a home for Shakespeare's work, the wider
classical repertoire and new plays.

The founding Artistic Director, Peter Hall, created an ensemble
theatre company of young actors and writers. The Company was led
by Hall, Peter Brook and Michel Saint-Denis. The founding principles
were threefold: the Company would embrace the freedom and power
of Shakespeare's work, train and develop young actors and
directors, and crucially, experiment in new ways of making theatre.
There was a new spirit amongst this post-war generation and they
intended to open up Shakespeare's plays as never before.

The impact of Peter Hall's vision cannot be underplayed. In 1955 he
had premiered Samuel Beckett's *Waiting for Godot* in London, and
the result was like opening a window during a storm. The tumult of
new ideas emerging across Europe in art, theatre and literature came
flooding into British theatre. Hall channelled this new excitement into
the setting up of the Company in Stratford. Exciting breakthroughs
took place in the rehearsal room and the studio day after day. The
RSC became known for exhilarating performances of Shakespeare
alongside new masterpieces such as *The Homecoming* and *Old
Times* by Harold Pinter. It was a combination that thrilled audiences.

Peter Hall's rigour on classical text became legendary, but what is little
known is that he applied everything he learned working on Beckett,
and later on Harold Pinter, to his work on Shakespeare, and likewise
he applied everything he learned from Shakespeare onto modern
texts. This close and exacting relationship between writers from
different eras became the fuel which powered the creativity of the RSC.

The search for new forms of writing and directing was led by Peter
Brook. He pushed writers to experiment. "Just as Picasso set out to

capture a larger slice of the truth by painting a face with several eyes and noses, Shakespeare, knowing that man is living his everyday life and at the same time is living intensely in the invisible world of his thoughts and feelings, developed a method through which we can see at one and the same time the look on a man's face and the vibrations of his brain."

A rich and varied range of writers flowed into the company and continue to do so. These include: Edward Albee, Howard Barker, Edward Bond, Howard Brenton, Marina Carr, Caryl Churchill, Martin Crimp, David Edgar, Peter Flannery, David Greig, Tony Harrison, Dennis Kelly, Martin McDonagh, Rona Munro, Anthony Neilson, Harold Pinter, Stephen Poliakoff, Adriano Shaplin, Wole Soyinka, Tom Stoppard, debbie tucker green, Timberlake Wertenbaker and Roy Williams.

The Company today is led by Michael Boyd, who is taking its founding ideals forward. His belief in ensemble theatre-making, internationalism, new work and active approaches to Shakespeare in the classroom has inspired the Company to landmark projects such as *The Complete Works Festival*, *Stand up for Shakespeare* and *The Histories Cycle*. He has overseen the four year transformation of our theatres, he has restored the full range of repertoire and in this birthday year we are proud to invite the world's theatre artists onto our brand new stages.

The RSC New Work season at Hampstead Theatre is generously supported by THE BLAVATNIK FAMILY FOUNDATION

The RSC Literary Department is generously supported by THE DRUE HEINZ TRUST

The RSC Ensemble is generously supported by THE GATSBY CHARITABLE FOUNDATION and THE KOVNER FOUNDATION

The RSC is grateful for the significant support of its principal funder, Arts Council England, without which our work would not be possible. Around 50 per cent of the RSC's income is self-generated from Box Office sales, sponsorship, donations, enterprise and partnerships with other organisations.

Supported by
ARTS COUNCIL ENGLAND

NEW WORK AT THE RSC

As well as commissioning plays each year from writers we love, we have recently re-launched the RST Studio to provide the resources for writers, directors and actors to explore and develop new ideas for our stages. We also explore the canon for classics to revive and lost classics to re-discover.

We invite writers to spend time with us in our rehearsal rooms, with our actors and practitioners. Alongside developing their own plays, we invite them to contribute dramaturgically to both our main stage Shakespeare productions and our Young People's Shakespeare.

We believe that our writers help to establish a creative culture within the Company which both inspires new work and creates an ever more urgent sense of enquiry into the classics. The benefits work both ways. With our writers, our actors naturally learn the language of dramaturgical intervention and sharpen their interpretation of roles. Our writers benefit from re-discovering the stagecraft and theatre skills that have been lost over time. They regain the knack of writing roles for leading actors. They become hungry to use classical structures to power up their plays.

Our current International Writer-in-Residence, Tarell Alvin McCraney, has been embedded with the company for two years. His post was funded by the CAPITAL Centre at the University of Warwick where he taught as part of his residency.

This production of *American Trade* was first performed by the Royal Shakespeare Company at Hampstead Theatre, London, on 2nd June 2011. The cast was as follows:

SHERMAN KANDEREBITZ	**Adam Burton**
LONI	**David Carr**
SENATOR ATWATER/LORD FAIRWAY	**Geoffrey Freshwater**
QWIK	**Gruffudd Glyn**
PHARUS	**Tunji Kasim**
GIRL WONDER	**Debbie Korley**
RAGIV	**Dharmesh Patel**
AUNT MARIAN	**Sheila Reid**
CABBIE	**David Rubin**
VALENTINA	**Sophie Russell**
SYLVIA	**Simone Saunders**
JULES	**Clarence Smith**
OFFICER JEFF	**James Traherne**
INTERVIEWER/OFFICER PERCY	**James Tucker**
BENTON	**Larrington Walker**
SVETLANA	**Kirsty Woodward**
SNOOTY LADY	**Hannah Young**
RED	**Samantha Young**

All other parts played by members of the Company

Directed by	**Jamie Lloyd**
Designed by	**Soutra Gilmour**
Lighting Designed by	**Neil Austin**
Music and Sound by	**Ben and Max Ringham**
Movement by	**Ann Yee**
Fights by	**Kate Waters**
Company Dramaturg	**Jeanie O'Hare**
Company Text and Voice Work	**Alison Bomber**
Dialect Coach	**Charmian Hoare**
Assistant Director	**Vik Sivalingam**
Music Director	**Nigel Lilley**
Casting by	**Hannah Miller**
	and Janine Snape CDG
Production Manager	**Rebecca Watts**
Costume Supervisor	**Chris Cahill**
Company Manager	**Michael Dembowicz**
Stage Manager	**Suzanne Bourke**
Deputy Stage Manager	**Gabrielle Sanders**
Assistant Stage Manager	**Christie Gerrard**

This text may differ slightly from the play as performed

Production Acknowledgments

Set built by Capital Scenery Limited. Graffiti artwork painted by artist Ser, Darren Cullen of Graffiti Kings, London. Properties by RSC workshops, Stratford-upon-Avon. Costume by Gill McGregor and Christopher Beales. Hip hop advisor, Duwane Taylor. Production photographer, Manuel Harlan. Audio description by Ellie Packer and Mary Plackett. Captioned by Janet Jackson.

THE COMPANY

NEIL AUSTIN
LIGHTING DESIGNER
RSC: *King Lear*, *The Seagull*, *Much Ado About Nothing*, *King John*, *Romeo and Juliet*, *Two Gentlemen of Verona* and *Julius Caesar*.
this season: *American Trade*.
other theatre includes: Winner of the 2011 Olivier Award for *The White Guard* at the National Theatre and the 2010 Tony and Drama Desk Awards for *Red* at the Golden Theatre on Broadway. *The Cherry Orchard*, *Women Beware Women*, *The White Guard*, *London Assurance*, *England People Very Nice*, *Oedipus*, *Her Naked Skin*, *Philistines*, *The Man of Mode*, *Thérèse Raquin*, *The Seafarer*, *Henry IV Parts 1 & 2* and *A Prayer for Owen Meany* (National Theatre); *The 25th Annual Putnam County Spelling Bee*, *King Lear*, *Passion*, *Red*, *A Streetcar Named Desire*, *Piaf*, *Parade*, *John Gabriel Borkman*, *Frost/Nixon*, *The Wild Duck*, *Caligula* and *After Miss Julie* (Donmar); *Betty Blue Eyes*, *The Children's Hour*, *Dealer's Choice*, *No Man's Land*, *A Life in the Theatre* and *Hamlet*, *Madame de Sade* and *Twelfth Night* (Donmar/West End).
dance includes: *Cinderella* (New Adventures); *As One* & *Rhapsody* (Royal Ballet).

ADAM BURTON

SHERMAN KANDEREBITZ
Ensemble productions: Sicilian Lord in *The Winter's Tale*, Metellus Cimber/Titinius in *Julius Caesar*, 1st Subordinate/2nd Policeman/2nd Ilya in *The Drunks*, Knight/Messenger/Captain in *King Lear*, Scarus in *Antony and Cleopatra*, Sherman Kanderebitz in *American Trade*.
trained: LIPA.
theatre includes: *Timon of Athens*, *A Midsummer Night's Dream* (Shakespeare's Globe); *Masque of the Red Death*, *Faust* (Punchdrunk); *As You Like It* (Derby Playhouse); *Baggage* (Pleasance); *The Adding Machine* (Rogue State/Courtyard); *The Waiting Game* (Courtyard/King's Head); *Heart of a Dog* (Rogue State/Assembly Rooms); *Blood Brothers* (No.1 tour); *Gogol's Underdogs* (Rogue State/The Underbelly).

television includes: *Doctors*, *Jekyll*, *Casualty*, *Harry on the Boat*, *Dangerfield*, *Treflan* (Welsh BAFTA winner).
film includes: *The Butcher's Shop* (Open Award winner at Venice Film Festival), *Short/Film* (best short film nomination at Austin Film Festival), *Breaker* (best short film nomination at Golden Lion Film Festival).

DAVID CARR

LONI
Ensemble productions: Charles in *As You Like It*, Egeon in *The Comedy of Errors*, Railway Worker/Vassiliev in *The Drunks*, Escalus in *Romeo and Juliet*, King Leodegrance/Accolon in *Morte d'Arthur*, Loni in *American Trade*.
trained: Central School of Speech and Drama.
theatre includes: *King Lear*, *Original Sin* (Sheffield Crucible); *Antony and Cleopatra*, *48-98*, *Brother to Brother* (Talawa Theatre Co.); *Macbeth*, *Deadmeat*,

The Comedy of Errors, Two Tracks and Text Me (West Yorkshire Playhouse); *One Flew Over the Cuckoo's Nest* (New Vic); *Futurology* (Suspect Culture/ Scottish National Theatre); *Romeo and Juliet* (Hayworth Theatre Co.).
television includes: *The Bill, A Touch of Frost, Soldier Soldier, Casualty, The Family Man, Living It, Doctors*.
film: *Greenstreet*.
radio includes: *Beau Carnival, Freefall, Speaking in Tongues*.

GEOFFREY FRESHWATER

SENATOR ATWATER/ LORD FAIRWAY
RSC: *The Histories Cycle, The Taming of the Shrew, Julius Caesar, The Merchant of Venice, The Changeling, Coriolanus, Happy End, The Odyssey, Much Ado About Nothing, Richard III, The Winter's Tale, King John, Jubilee, The Malcontent, The Roman Actor, Eastward Ho!, Thomas More, A New Way To Please You, Sejanus: His Fall*.

Ensemble productions: Corin in *As You Like It*, Landowner in *The Grain Store*, Earl of Gloucester in *King Lear*, Agrippa in *Antony and Cleopatra*, Senator Atwater/Lord Fairway in *American Trade*.
theatre includes: *The Barber of Seville, The Tempest, The Way of the World, Dracula, Arsenic and Old Lace* (Chichester); *The Faerie Queen* (Aix-en-Provence); *The Invisible Man* (Stratford East); *The Churchill Play, The Mother, The Merry Wives of Windsor, The Alchemist* (National Theatre); *Once in a Lifetime* (Piccadilly); *Piaf* (Wyndham's).
television includes: *The Professionals, Poirot, No Bananas, Trial and Retribution, Foyle's War, The Commander, Midsomer Murders, The Government Inspector*.
film includes: *A Bridge Too Far, The Grotesque, The Leading Man, Nocturnal, Sabotage*.
radio includes: *Patricia's Progress, Friends of Oscar, Top Story*.

SOUTRA GILMOUR

DESIGNER
RSC: *The Tragedy of Thomas Hobbes*.
this season: *American Trade*.
trained: Wimbledon School of Arts.
theatre includes: *In a Forest Dark and Deep* (Vaudeville); *Into The Woods* (Regents Park Open Air Theatre); *Piaf* (Donmar/ Vaudeville/Buenos Aires); *Polar Bears* (Donmar); *The Little Dog Laughed* (Garrick); *Three Days of Rain* (Apollo); *The Pride* (Royal Court); *The Lover and The Collection* (Comedy); *Our Friends in the North, Ruby Moon, Son of Man* (Northern Stage); *Last Easter* (Birmingham Rep); *Angels in America* (Lyric Hammersmith); *Bad Jazz, Brief History of Helen of Troy* (ATC); *The Birthday Party* (Sheffield Crucible); *The Caretaker* (Sheffield Crucible/Tricycle); *Petrol Jesus Nightmare # 5* (Traverse/Kosovo); *Lovers & War* (Stockholm); *Hair, Witness* (Gate); *Baby Doll, Thérèse Raquin* (Citizens, Glasgow); *Ghost City* (New York); *When the World was Green* (Young Vic); *Modern Dance for Beginners* (Soho); *Through the Leaves* (Duchess/Southwark Playhouse); *Shadow of a Boy* (National Theatre).

opera includes:
OperaShots, Down by the Greenwood Side/Into the Little Hill (Royal Opera House); *Anna Bolena, Don Giovanni, Così fan tutte, Mary Stuart* (English Touring Opera); *The Shops* (Bregenz Festival); *The Birds, Trouble in Tahiti* (The Opera Group); *El Cimmamon* (Queen Elizabeth Hall); *Saul, Hansel & Gretel* (Opera North); *A Better Place* (English National Opera); *Girl of Sand* (Almeida).

GRUFFUDD GLYN

QWIK
Ensemble productions:
Young Shepherd in *The Winter's Tale*, Cinna/Young Cato in *Julius Caesar*, Todos in *The Grain Store*, Barnardo/Guildenstern/Osric in *Hamlet*, Balthasar in *Romeo and Juliet*, Gareth in *Morte d'Arthur*, Qwik in *American Trade*.
trained: RADA (winner of the Richard Burton Scholarship award).
theatre: *Romeo and Juliet* (Middle Temple Hall).

CHARMIAN HOARE

DIALECT COACH
RSC: *The Winter's Tale*.
trained: Central School of Speech and Drama.
this season: *Silence, American Trade*.
Charmian has worked extensively in theatre and film as a Voice and Dialect coach. She has also worked for many years at the Guildhall School of Music and Drama and is now a professor at Pennsylvania State University, USA, teaching there every autumn.
other theatre includes:
Brighton Beach Memoirs (Watford Palace); *I Oughta be in Pictures* (Manchester Library); *Dancing at Lughnasa, Arthur and George* (Birmingham Rep); *Under Milk Wood, The Grapes of Wrath* (Colchester Mercury); *Death of a Salesman, Deep Blue Sea* (West Yorkshire Playhouse); *The Crucible* (Regents Park Open Air Theatre); *Jerusalem, Red Bud* (Royal Court); *Love Story, Goodnight Mr Tom* (Chichester Festival); *View from a Bridge, Hayfever, The Blue Room* (Theatre by the Lake, Keswick); *The Big Fellah* (Out of Joint); *Hamlet* (Crucible); *Desire Under the Elms, Bus Stop* (New Vic, Stoke on Trent); *The House of Games* (Almeida); *Novecento* (Donmar); *Blithe Spirit, Masterclass* (Theatre Royal, Bath); *The Mountaintop, Precious Little Talent* (Trafalgar Studios); *Ghost the Musical* (Opera House, Manchester).

TUNJI KASIM

PHARUS
Ensemble productions:
Florizel in *The Winter's Tale*, Romulus/Lucius in *Julius Caesar*, Arsei Pechoritsa in *The Grain Store*, Edmund in *King Lear*, Mardian/Sentry in *Antony and Cleopatra*, Pharus in *American Trade*.
trained: Royal Scottish Academy of Music and Drama.
theatre includes: *The Brothers Size* (ATC/Young Vic); *The Cracks in My Skin* (Royal Exchange); *Big White Fog* (Almeida); *The Dutchman* (Arcola).
television: *Nearly Famous*.

DEBBIE KORLEY

GIRL WONDER
Ensemble productions:
Hisperia in *As You Like It*,
Luciana in *The Comedy of
Errors*, Gafiika in *The Grain
Store*, Ophelia/Pirate in
Hamlet, Lady in *Romeo and
Juliet*, Nimue in *Morte
d'Arthur*, Rita/Natasha in
Little Eagles, Girl Wonder in
American Trade.
theatre includes: *Coram
Boy, A Matter of Life and
Death* (National Theatre);
Feathers in the Snow
(National Theatre Studio);
Cinderella (Theatre Royal,
Stratford East); *Whistle
Down the Wind* (West End/
tour); *Sick!* (Almeida); *Ten
Suitcases* (Drill Hall); *Aida*
(Royal Albert Hall); *Carmen
Jones* (Old Vic); *The Vagina
Monologues* (Mercury,
Colchester); *The Count of
Monte Cristo* (West Yorkshire
Playhouse); *Saturday Night*
(White Bear); *Annie*
(Edinburgh Festival/National
Youth Music Theatre).
television includes:
*Doctors, Casualty, Holy
Smoke, Night and Day,
Green Balloon Club*.

NIGEL LILLEY

MUSIC DIRECTOR
RSC debut season:
American Trade.
trained: King's College,
London and the Royal
Academy of Music, where
he was the recipient of the
DipRam award.
theatre includes: *The
Umbrellas of Cherbourg*
(Curve, Leicester/West End);
Sweet Charity (Menier
Chocolate Factory/Theatre
Royal, Haymarket); *The Rise
and Fall of Little Voice*
(Vaudeville); *Spring
Awakening* (Lyric
Hammersmith/Novello); *La
Cage aux Folles* (Menier
Chocolate
Factory/Playhouse); *Piaf,
Pacific Overtures* (Donmar);
The Bacchae (National
Theatre of Scotland); *Lauren
Kennedy in Concert* (Menier
Chocolate Factory); *The
Most Happy Fella* (London
workshop); *Les Misérables*
(Bournemouth Symphony
Orchestra); *Sinatra* (London
Palladium); *The Last Session*
(Hackney Empire Studio);
The Far Pavilions
(Shaftesbury); *Putting It
Together* (Harrogate); *Glitter
and Twisted* (Beckett
Theatre, New York); *Les
Misérables* (Denmark);
Maury Yeston's *December
Songs* (Greenwich); *Philip
Quast at the Donmar* (Divas
season).
other work includes: Nigel
has performed extensively

with Clare Burt in cabaret
and released an album
together, *Now You Know,* in
2010. He was involved with
the Channel 4 series,
Musicality, and has also
enjoyed regular
collaborations with Victoria
Wood on projects including
*The Giddy Kipper, Eric and
Ernie, Victoria Wood's
Christmas Special, Talent*
and *Acorn Antiques*. He is
co-author with Mary
Hammond, of the audition
handbook *Thank you, that's
all we need for today*
published by Edition Peters.
In spring 2011 Nigel was
elected as an Associate of
the Royal Academy of
Music.

JAMIE LLOYD

DIRECTOR
RSC debut season:
American Trade.
theatre includes: at the
Donmar: *The 25th Annual
Putnam County Spelling
Bee, Passion* (Evening
Standard Award for Best
Musical, Olivier nomination
for Best Musical Revival),
Polar Bears, Piaf (also
Vaudeville, Teatro Liceo
Buenos Aires and Teatro
Alcala Madrid; Olivier
nomination for Best Musical
Revival, Hugo Award for Best
Director, Clarin Award for
Best Musical Production),
Company (concert at the
Queens) and stage readings
of *A House Not Meant To*

Stand and *The Cocktail Party*. Other theatre: *Salome* (Headlong/Curve/Hampstead); *The Little Dog Laughed* (Garrick); *Three Days of Rain* (Apollo; Olivier nomination for Best Revival); *The Pride* (Royal Court; Olivier Award for Outstanding Achievement); *Eric's* (Liverpool Everyman); *The Lover* and *The Collection* (Comedy); *The Caretaker* (Sheffield Crucible/ Tricycle). Future projects include *The Faith Machine* (Royal Court); *Inadmissible Evidence* (Donmar); *She Stoops to Conquer* (National Theatre).

Jamie is an Associate Director of the Donmar and the Associate Artist at Headlong.

DHARMESH PATEL

RAGIV
Ensemble productions: Lord Amiens in *As You Like It*, Angelo in *The Comedy of Errors*, Onis'ko in *The Grain Store*, Hamlet in *Hamlet*, Gregory in *Romeo and Juliet*, Agravain/Lucifer in *Morte d'Arthur*, Ragiv in *American Trade*.

trained: Hope Street Physical Theatre School.
theatre includes: *Happy and Married?*, *Silent Cry* (Freedom Studios); *Satyagraha* (Improbable); *Beauty and the Beast*, *Accidental Death of an Anarchist* (Told by an Idiot); *Too Close to Home* (RASA); *Slowtime* (National Theatre); *The Happy Prince, Bollywood Jane* (Haymarket, Leicester); *No Fear, The Government Inspector, Beauty and the Beast* (Unity Theatre).
television includes: *Casualty, Doctors, Ray's Daze.*
radio includes: *Jefferson 37, Silver Street, Whimmy Road.*

SHEILA REID

AUNT MARIAN
RSC: *Romeo and Juliet*, *'Tis Pity She's a Whore*, *Richard III*.
this season: *American Trade*.
theatre includes: seven years with Laurence Olivier's Company including *Three Sisters, The Crucible, Much Ado About Nothing, The Beaux' Stratagem, Hedda Gabler* (National Theatre); *The Gentle Avalanche* (most promising actress award), *My Mother said I Never Should, Black Milk, Terrorism* (Royal Court); *When I was a Girl I used to Scream and Shout, The Girl with Red Hair* (Bush/Whitehall); *The Winter Guest* (Almeida); *The Importance of Being Earnest* (Chichester/Haymarket); *Pornography* (Tricycle). Sheila's own shows, *Love Among the Butterflies* and *Terrible with Raisins In It* sold out in Edinburgh and London.
musicals include: *Sweeney Todd* (National Theatre); *Into the Woods* (Donmar); *Martin Guerre* (Prince Edward); *On the Town* (ENO at the Theatre de Chatelet, Paris).
television includes: *Benidorm* (2 national television awards), *Justice, Your Mother Should Know, Place of Execution, A Room with a View, Sea of Souls, Taggart, Midsomer Murders, Doctors, Bones, Doctor Who.*
film includes: *Five Days One Summer, The Touch, Brazil, Winter Guest, The Lonely Passion of Judith Hearne, Othello, Three Sisters, Cabbage Wars.*

BEN & MAX RINGHAM

MUSIC AND SOUND DESIGN

RSC debut season: *Little Eagles, American Trade.*
other theatre includes: *Racing Demon, Hamlet, An Enemy of the People* (Sheffield Crucible); *Les Parents Terrible* (Donmar at Trafalgar Studios); *Electric Hotel* (Sadler's Wells/Fuel); *Salome* (Headlong); *The Man from Stratford* (Ambassadors); *Polar Bears* (Donmar); *The Little Dog Laughed* (Garrick); *Three Days of Rain* (Apollo, West End); *The Rise and Fall of Little Voice* (Vaudeville); *The Author, The Pride* (Royal Court); *Really Old Like Forty Five, Henry IV Parts I and II* (National Theatre); *Phaedra* (Donmar); *Piaf* (Donmar/ Vaudeville/Buenos Aires); *Branded, All About my Mother* (Old Vic); *Contains Violence* (Lyric Hammersmith); *The Lover/The Collection* (Comedy, West End); *The Caretaker* (Sheffield Crucible/Tricycle/ tour); *Amato Saltone, What If...? Tropicana, Dance Bear Dance, The Ballad of Bobby Francois* (Shunt); *The Pigeon* (BAC); Ben and Max won Best Overall Achievement in an Affiliate Theatre Olivier award for *The Pride.*
other work includes: Ben and Max are associate artists with the Shunt collective and two thirds of the band Superthriller.

DAVID RUBIN

CABBIE

RSC: *Antony and Cleopatra, Julius Caesar, The Tempest.*
Ensemble productions: Sicilian Lord in *The Winter's Tale*, Trebonius/ Lucilius in *Julius Caesar*, Yukhim in *The Grain Store*, Claudius in *Hamlet*, Montague in *Romeo and Juliet*, King Uriens/ Lucan/Stag in *Morte d'Arthur*, Cabbie in *American Trade.*
theatre includes: *Fightface* (Lyric Hammersmith); *As the Mother of a Brown Boy, Hamlet, The Attraction, Paula's Story* (Chickenshed); *The Overcoat, Taylor's Dummies* (Gecko); *The Red Balloon, Threepenny Opera, A Midsummer Night's Dream, As You Like It, The Tempest*, two productions of *Twelfth Night* (National Theatre); *Five Guys Named Moe* (Lyric); *In the Midnight Hour* (Young Vic); *Godspell* (Barbican); *Macbeth* (Chester Gateway); *Cyrano de Bergerac* (Theatre Royal, Northampton); *Company, Duck Variations* (New Wolsey, Ipswich); *The Legend of King Arthur* (Red Shift); *100* (The Imaginary Body); *Sharrow Stories* (Sheffield Crucible); *The Wizard of Oz* (Oldham Coliseum); *Peter Pan* (Nuffield, Southampton); *Stomp* (Royal Festival Hall).
television includes: *The Passion, Holby City, Walking With Cavemen, EastEnders, Dalziel and Pascoe, Sitting Pretty, Mysteries of July, Running Time, Number 73, Watch, Good Health, Playdays.*
film includes: *Brooms, Crossover, After a Time.*
David was a founder member of The Company at Chickenshed Theatre and is a Freelance Associate Practitioner for the RSC.

SOPHIE RUSSELL

VALENTINA

Ensemble productions: Audrey in *As You Like It*, Abbess in *The Comedy of Errors*, Plump Woman/ Woman in Beret in *The Drunks*, Fool in *King Lear*, Octavia in *Antony and Cleopatra*, Valentina in *American Trade.*
trained: Middlesex University, Ecole Nationale Superieure

des Arts et Techniques du Theatre, Paris.

theatre includes: *The Good Soul of Szechuan* (Young Vic); *Spyski!* (Peepolykus/ Lyric Hammersmith); *The Crock of Gold, Metamorphosis, Alice Through the Looking Glass, The Tinderbox* (London Bubble); *The Chaingang Gang, Meat and Two Veg, The Ratcatcher of Hamelin* (Cartoon de Salvo/BAC); *Invisible Town* (National Theatre Studio); *The Bitches' Ball* (Assembly Rooms, Edinburgh); *Great Expectations* (Shifting Sands Theatre Co.); *Oliver Twist* (International tour); *I Am Dandy* (David Gale Ensemble); *Cinderella* (Palace, Westcliff); *A Christmas Carol* (Palace, Newark).

television: *Wire in the Blood.*

SIMONE SAUNDERS

SYLVIA

RSC: *The Castle* (rehearsed reading).

Ensemble productions: Dorcas/Lady in *The Winter's*

Tale, Calphurnia's Servant in *Julius Caesar*, Mokrina's Sister/Nurse in *The Grain Store*, Horatio in *Hamlet*, Lady Montague in *Romeo and Juliet*, Queen Igraine/ Lynet in *Morte d'Arthur*, Sylvia in *American Trade*.

trained: East 15.

theatre includes: *Claudia Jones* (Talawa Theatre); *The Tempest* (Northern Broadsides); *Double Take* (Nottingham Playhouse/Red Earth); *The Red Ladies* (Clod Ensemble/National Theatre); *Goodnight Desdemona, Good Morning Juliet* (Toucan Theatre Co.).

VIK SIVALINGAM

ASSISTANT DIRECTOR
RSC: *Romeo and Juliet.*
Ensemble productions: *The Comedy of Errors, The Grain Store, King Lear, American Trade.*

trained: Birkbeck, University of London.

theatre includes: As Director: *The Bullet* (Hampstead); *Once On This Island, Daisy Pulls It Off* (Cockpit); *Platform* (Old Vic New Voices); *The Death of Tintagel* (Peoples Show Theatre); *Uncle Vanya* (Sturdy Beggars Theatre Company); *Ballet Russes* (A Stage Kindly Productions); *Stuff* (Tristan Bates Theatre); *Or Nearest Offer* (Almeida); *Three Sisters* (Actors

Company); *Elephant Man* (Associate Director, Sheffield Theatres tour); *Jack and the Beanstalk* (Gatehouse, Stafford); *When The Lights Went Out* (Tara Arts), *Human Rights* (Sir John Mills Theatre, Ipswich); *Blue/ Orange* (New Wolsey Theatre Studio); *Day Trippers* (New Wolsey Theatre/Theatr Clwyd). As Assistant Director: *Free Outgoing* (Royal Court); *The Last Days of Judas Iscariot* (Almeida); *Rough Crossings* (Headlong); *The Soldier's Fortune* (Young Vic); *The Price, Private Lives, The Tempest, Sugar* (New Wolsey).

CLARENCE SMITH

JULES

RSC: *Noughts & Crosses, The Winter's Tale, Pericles, King Lear, Don Juan.*

Ensemble productions: Duke Ferdinand in *As You Like It*, 3rd Babitsky/1st Policeman in *The Drunks*, Duke of Cornwall in *King*

Lear, Pompey in *Antony and Cleopatra*, Jules in *American Trade*.

theatre includes: *King Lear* (Headlong); *Pure Gold, Shrieks of Laughter* (Soho); *Design for Living, Les Blancs* (Royal Exchange); *Macbeth* (Arcola); *The Storm* (Almeida); *As You Like It* (Tokyo Globe); *The Honest Whore, The Merchant of Venice* (Shakespeare's Globe); *King Lear, Chasing the Moment* (Southwark Playhouse); *Romeo and Juliet, Fuente Ovejuna, Yerma, Blood Brothers, Hiawatha* (Bristol Old Vic); *The Jamaican Airman Foresees his Death, Our Country's Good, Charity Event* (Royal Court).

television includes: *Doctors, The Last Detective, Holby City, The Eustace Bros, Waking the Dead, EastEnders, Undercover Cops, Daylight Robbery, The Bill, Sharman*.

film includes: *Mexican Standoff, Star Wars, The Dinner, What my Mother Told Me*.

other work includes: *The Remnant, Johnny was a Good Man* (writer/director), *Ragamuffin, Some Kind of Hero* (director/co-producer) (Double Edge).

JAMES TRAHERNE

OFFICER JEFF
Ensemble productions: Sir Oliver Martext in *As You Like It*, Solinus in *The Comedy of Errors*, Efremov in *The Drunks*, Sampson/ Watchman in *Romeo and Juliet*, King Lot/Red Knight/Bedevere in *Morte d'Arthur*, Officer Jeff in *American Trade*.

trained: Rose Bruford College.

theatre includes: *The Venetian Twins* (Bolton Octagon); *Rapunzel* (Kneehigh at Queen Elizabeth Hall/Broadway); *The Car Cemetery* (Gate); *Martin Guerre, The Thieves Carnival* (Watermill); *The Soldier's Fortune* (Young Vic); *Tristan and Yseult* (Kneehigh at Sydney/ Wellington Festival); *Twelfth Night, The Hired Man* (Theatre by the Lake); *Caledonian Road* (Almeida); *Junk* (Bristol Old Vic); *Johnny Blue* (Oxford Stage Co.); *Gulliver* (Riverside

Studios); *Nicholas Nickleby* (Red Shift); *Holes* (Stratford East).

television includes: *Clone, Supergrass, Go Now, The Bill, Dream Team, Jenner, Jump.*

film includes: *The Mummy, Over Exposed, The Sobering.*

JAMES TUCKER

INTERVIEWER/ OFFICER PERCY
RSC: *The Histories Cycle, Eastward Ho!, The Malcontent, Edward III, The Island Princess, Henry VI Parts I, II and III, Richard III, The Lion, the Witch and the Wardrobe, The Two Gentlemen of Verona, Bartholomew Fair, Measure for Measure, Seeds Under Stones, A Woman of No Importance.*

Ensemble productions: Silvius in *As You Like It*, Antipholus of Ephesus in *The Comedy of Errors*, Rudenko in *The Grain Store*, Oswald in *King Lear*, Maecenas in *Antony and Cleopatra*, Interviewer/

Officer Percy in *American Trade*.
theatre includes: *Ivanov* (Donmar Warehouse at Wyndham's); *The Winter's Tale, Twelfth Night, Henry V* (Propeller at the Watermill Theatre. UK and world tours); *Hamlet* (UK tour); *A Midsummer Night's Dream* (Sheffield Crucible); *Hinge of the World* (Yvonne Arnaud); *The Cherry Orchard* (English Touring Theatre); *The Tempest* (Nottingham Playhouse/world tour); *Hamlet* (Glasgow Citizens); *Twelfth Night* (Nottingham Playhouse); *Shadowlands* (national tour); *A Month in the Country* (Albery).
television includes: *Agatha Christie: A Life in Pictures, Silent Witness*.

LARRINGTON WALKER

BENTON
RSC: *The Merchant of Venice, The Taming of the Shrew, The Tragedy of Thomas Hobbes*.
Ensemble productions: Old Shepherd in *The Winter's Tale*, Soothsayer/

Octavius' Servant/Strato in *Julius Caesar*, Feodosii/ Guard in *The Grain Store*, Knight/Old Man in *King Lear*, Alexas in *Antony and Cleopatra*, Benton in *American Trade*.
theatre includes: *Jenufa* (Arcola); *Daddy Cool* (Shaftesbury/Berlin); *Ska Ba Day* (Greenwich/Talawa); *Pinocchio, Old Time Story* (Theatre Royal, Stratford East); *Playboy of the West Indies* (Tricycle/Nottingham); *Stuff Happens, The Beggar's Opera, Guys and Dolls* (National Theatre); *Blues for Mr. Charlie* (Wolsey/Tricycle); *Driving Miss Daisy* (Oldham Coliseum); *Wrong Time Right Place* (Soho Theatre Co.); *Whistle Down the Wind* (tour); *The Free State* (Birmingham Rep/ tour); *The Merchant of Venice* (West Yorkshire Playhouse); *Lost in the Stars* (New Sussex Opera, Brighton); *Week In Week Out* (Foco Novo/Soho Poly); *Jesus Christ Superstar* (Palace Theatre).
television includes: *The Bill, Beck, Peak Practice, Inspector Morse, Playdays, Tecx, You and Me, Thin Air, Waterloo Sunset, Murder Rap, Chinese Detective, Minder*.
film includes: *Human Traffic, Lamb, Burning Illusion, Yanks*.
radio includes: *Equiano, Whose is the Kingdom?, Rudy's Rare Records*.

KATE WATERS

FIGHT DIRECTOR
Ensemble productions: *King Lear, American Trade*.
recent theatre includes: *Frankenstein, Season's Greetings, Hamlet, Women Beware Women, Mrs. Affleck, Every Good Boy Deserves Favour* (National Theatre); *Othello* (West Yorkshire Playhouse/Trafalgar Studios); *Kes* (Liverpool Playhouse); *Apple Cart, Bedroom Farce* (for Peter Hall), *How the Other Half Loves, Moonlight & Magnolias* (Stephen Joseph, Scarborough); *War Horse* (National Theatre/New London Theatre); *Spring Awakening* (Lyric Hammersmith/ Novello); *A Midsummer Night's Dream, A Chorus of Disapproval* (Theatre by the Lake, Keswick); *Entertaining Mr Sloane* (Trafalgar Studios); *His Dark Materials* (Birmingham Rep); *Any Which Way* (Only Connect, London); *The Pride* (Royal Court); *The Lion, the Witch and the Wardrobe* (West Yorkshire Playhouse/ Birmingham Rep); *See How they Run* (Manchester Royal Exchange); *Romeo and Juliet* (Theatre of Memory); *Turandot, What Fatima Did* (Hampstead); *Great Expectations* (New Vic, Newcastle-Under-Lyme); *As You Like It* (Watford Palace); *Hamlet* (Tobacco Factory, Bristol).

television: *Coronation Street.*

Kate is one of only two women on the Equity Register of Fight Directors.

KIRSTY WOODWARD

SVETLANA

Ensemble productions: Mopsa/Lady in *The Winter's Tale*, Priestess in *Julius Caesar*, Kilina in *The Grain Store*, Gertrude in *Hamlet*, Lady in *Romeo and Juliet*, Guenever in *Morte d'Arthur*, Svetlana in *American Trade*.

trained: National Youth Theatre and Kneehigh Theatre.

theatre includes: *Beauty and the Beast* (Told by an Idiot/Warwick Arts Centre). With Kneehigh Theatre: *Cymbeline* (RSC Complete Works Festival/Lyric Hammersmith/tour), *Rapunzel* (BAC/Queen Elizabeth Hall), *A Matter of Life and Death* (National Theatre), *Blast* (national tour).

ANN YEE

MOVEMENT DIRECTOR

RSC: *King Lear.*

this season: *American Trade.*

As choreographer / movement director: *The Secret Garden* (West Yorkshire Playhouse); *Shraddha, This Isn't Romance* (Soho); *Mates* (Latitude Festival - Drywrite); *Much Ado about Nothing* (Regent's Park Open Air Theatre); *Eric's* (Liverpool Everyman); *Romeo and Juliet* (Middle Temple Hall); *Oxford Street* (Royal Court); *Hamlet* (Theater Rozmaitosci, Warsaw); *The Lion, the Witch and the Wardrobe* (West Yorkshire Playhouse/Birmingham Rep); *Bad Girls the Musical* (Garrick); *Angels in America* (Lyric Hammersmith/UK tour); *Bent* (Trafalgar Studios); *Hair, Big Love* (Gate); *Woyzeck* (St Anne's Warehouse, New York/Gate); *The Odyssey* (Lyric Hammersmith/Bristol Old Vic); *The Magic Carpet* (Lyric Hammersmith); *Food* (Traverse/UK tour); *Sex, Chips and Rock and Roll* (Royal Exchange).

HANNAH YOUNG

SNOOTY LADY

RSC: *The Merry Wives of Windsor, Coriolanus* (RSC/Old Vic), *The Lion, the Witch and the Wardrobe* (Sadler's Wells).

Ensemble productions: Emilia in *The Winter's Tale*, Portia in *Julius Caesar*, Natasha in *The Drunks*, Nurse in *King Lear*, Charmian in *Antony and Cleopatra*, Anna/Xenia in *Little Eagles*, Snooty Lady in *American Trade*.

trained: University of Exeter.

theatre includes: *Corporate Rock* (Nabokov); *The Lady from the Sea* (Birmingham Rep); *Songs of Grace and Redemption* (Theatre503); *The French Lieutenant's Woman* (Yvonne Arnaud/No.1 tour); *As You Desire* (Playhouse, West End); *Time and the Conways* (Theatre Royal Bath/No.1 tour); *First Love, Kishon Brook* (International

Playwrighting Festival, Royal Court; *A Chaste Maid in Cheapside* (Almeida/No.1 tour); *Les Liaisons Dangereuses* (Liverpool Playhouse); *A Midsummer Night's Dream* (Albery, West End); *The Importance of Being Earnest* (Deptford Albany); *Queer Dorset Bastard* (Camden Etcetera); *The Stringless Marionette* (Orange Tree); *The Swell* (Theatre Alibi).
television includes: *Britain's Nazi King, Doctors, The Robinsons, Waking the Dead, Offenders.*
film: *Alan's Breakfast.*
radio: *Levitt in London.*

Citizens); *Europe* (Dundee Rep/Barbican); *Gobbo, Miss Julie, The Crucible* (National Theatre of Scotland); *A Taste of Honey* (Glasgow Citizens); *The Graduate, The Visit, A Lie of the Mind, Macbeth* (Dundee Rep); *Snow White* (Glasgow Citizens).
television includes: *Casualty, River City.*
short film: *Mono.*
radio includes: *Freefalling, Look Back in Anger, Almost Blue.*

SAMANTHA YOUNG

RED
RSC: *I'll be the Devil.*
Ensemble productions: Perdita in *The Winter's Tale*, Soothsayer's Acolyte in *Julius Caesar*, Mokrina Staritskaya in *The Grain Store*, Cordelia in *King Lear*, Iras in *Antony and Cleopatra*, Valya in *Little Eagles*, Red in *American Trade*.
trained: RSAMD.
theatre includes: *Videotape* (Oran Mor); *Fall* (Traverse, Edinburgh); *Hamlet* (Glasgow

JOIN US

Join us from £18 a year.

Join today and make a difference

The Royal Shakespeare Company is an ensemble. We perform all year round in our Stratford-upon-Avon home, as well as having regular seasons in London, and touring extensively within the UK and overseas for international residencies.

With a range of options from £18 to £10,000 per year, there are many ways to engage with the RSC.

Choose a level that suits you and enjoy a closer connection with us whilst also supporting our work on stage.

Find us online

Sign up for regular email updates at **www.rsc.org.uk/signup**

Join today

Annual RSC Full Membership costs just £40 (or £18 for Associate Membership) and provides you with regular updates on RSC news, advance information and priority booking.

Support us

A charitable donation from £100 a year can offer you the benefits of membership, whilst also allowing you the opportunity to deepen your relationship with the Company through special events, backstage tours and exclusive ticket booking services.

The options include Shakespeare's Circle (from £100), Patrons' Circle (Silver: £1,000, Gold: £5,000) and Artists' Circle (£10,000).

For more information visit **www.rsc.org.uk/joinus** or call the RSC Membership Office on 01789 403 440.

THE ROYAL SHAKESPEARE COMPANY

Hampstead Theatre is one of the UK's leading new writing companies – a company that has just celebrated its fiftieth year of operation.

Throughout its long history the theatre has existed to support a thriving local, national and international playwriting culture. We commission plays in order to enrich and enliven this culture. We support, develop and produce the work of new writers, emerging writers, established writers, mid-career writers and senior writers and have a proud tradition for creating the conditions for their plays and careers to develop.

The list of playwrights who had their early work produced at Hampstead Theatre and who are now filling theatres all over the country and beyond include Mike Leigh, Michael Frayn, Brian Friel, Terry Johnson, Hanif Kureishi, Simon Block, Abi Morgan, Rona Munro, Tamsin Oglesby, Harold Pinter, Shelagh Stephenson, debbie tucker green, Crispin Whittell, Roy Williams and Dennis Kelly.

The Creative Learning programme is also an integral part of Hampstead Theatre's work. We aim to celebrate all aspects of the creative process in ways which support learning and widen access to the theatre's programme. Inspiring creativity and developing emerging talent, at its best our work has the power to change lives.

In January 2010, Edward Hall was appointed Artistic Director of Hampstead Theatre. Hall's inaugural season was a box office success culminating in a West End transfer of Mike Leigh's revival of *Ecstasy*. Hampstead Theatre looks forward to welcoming the RSC and Hall's own company, the internationally acclaimed Propeller, over the forthcoming months.

Hampstead Downstairs was opened in November 2010. It seats 98 and stages raw, edgy and experimental work. The audience decide for themselves what they think of the work, with their decisions not being predetermined by media reviews. Previous productions include *small hours* directed by Katie Mitchell and *.45* written by Gary Lennon.

Hall's second season, autumn 2011, will continue to delight, inspire and engage with such directors as Katie Mitchell, Richard Eyre and Roger Michell taking to the stage.

Hampstead Theatre, Eton Avenue, Swiss Cottage, London NW3 3EU
www.hampsteadtheatre.com

Supported by
ARTS COUNCIL ENGLAND

Registered charity number: 218506

Tarell Alvin McCraney

Tarell trained at the Yale School of Drama. He is the newest ensemble member at the Steppenwolf Theater Company, Chicago, a member of Teo Castellanos/ D Projects in Miami, and in residence at New Dramatists, New York. His 'Brother/Sister Plays' form a sequence comprising *In the Red and Brown Water* (Alliance Theatre, Atlanta; Young Vic, London), *The Brothers Size* (Studio Theater, DC; Public Theater, New York, with the Foundry Theater; Abbey Theatre, Dublin; McCarter Theater, Princeton; Young Vic with ATC, London) and *Marcus or the Secret of Sweet* (premiered in a co-production by McCarter Theater and the Public Theater). The 'Brother/ Sister Plays' have also been staged by Steppenwolf, the American Conservatory Theatre, Seattle Rep, Marin Theater Company, the Magic Theater, and the Guthrie Theater. His other plays include *Wig Out!* (presented at the Vineyard Theater, New York, and the Royal Court, London), *Without/Sin*, *Run Mourner Run* and *The Breach*, written with Catherine Filloux and Joe Sutton. For the Royal Shakespeare Company, he has directed the production of *Hamlet* in the Young People's Shakespeare season.

also by Tarell Alvin McCraney

THE BROTHERS SIZE
IN THE RED AND BROWN WATER
WIG OUT!

Tarell Alvin McCraney
American Trade

A CONTEMPORARY
RESTORATION COMEDY

a part of the
Identity Plays

faber and faber

First published in 2011
by Faber and Faber Limited
74–77 Great Russell Street, London WC1B 3DA

Typeset by Country Setting, Kingsdown, Kent CT14 8ES
Printed by CPI Group (UK) Ltd, Croydon, CR0 4YY

A CIP record for this book
is available from the British Library

ISBN 978-0-571-28051-3

For L^2

Special thanks to

Capital Centre at Warwick University, Coventry, UK,
McCarter Theater in Princeton, NJ, and Chris Myers,
Jeanie O'Hare and Jamie 'Jam-Roc' Lloyd

Characters

Pharus

Loni

Jules

Aunt Marian

Girl Wonder

Senator Atwater

Sherman Kanderebitz

Interviewer

Sylvia Watson

Valentina

Qwik

Snooty Lady

Lord Fairway

Ragiv

Officer Percy

Officer Jeff

Red

Cabbie

Svetlana (Slenda)

Benton

Act One

Pharus's apartment.

Pharus
LIGHTS!
SLAP PUNCH GRAB.

Loni slaps, punches, and then grabs Pharus.

Loni
Motherfucker!

Jules
You serious? Are you kidding me? Do you know who
I am?

Loni
You know who he is?

Jules
I'm Me!

Loni
The Jules Mac Mana!

Pharus
But I'm telling you that's the truth, Jules.

Jules
Pharus, come on. Come on! You expect me to believe . . .
Let me explain this to you. I'm the cover of that damn
company. Ditch Diggin' Records is built off the hits
I put together. The young talent I scouted, the money
I made it. The parent company, the bigwig dudes who
sit back and make money, they don't want no parts
of the day-in and day-outs. They leave that shit to me.

So you have to excuse my up-and-down-round-and-round surprise.
I walk in the studio . . .

Loni
Built off his back.

Jules
And find the CEO of the company sitting with his feet up on the soundboard.

Loni
Like he own the place.

Jules
And I want him to get gone.
I put on the good Negro face for him.
Hey man, what can I do for you?

Loni
'Oh, well, I'm looking for Pharus!'

Jules
Who!

Loni
Pharus!

Jules
You talking about 'Tag-along Pharus?'
'Just-met-him-a-month-or-so-ago Pharus?'
Why is this man in my place of employment looking for you, Pharus?

Pharus
I told you, I said hello to him in the elevator one day.

Jules
Oh is that all?
Hold him up!

Pharus
BACK UP!

Loni jacks Pharus up.

Jules

You talking about a man I ain't seen since I was rocking a fro.

Loni

Ain't got no hair now.

Jules

And he sitting on my soundboard in my office waiting to see you because you said hello to him in the elevator? Look more like he and you got an appointment. What could you possibly have to talk to my boss about?

Pharus

I . . . I'm going to be real with you, Jules.

Jules

Oh that's lovely, Pharus, that's . . . that's what I want, 'real'.

Pharus

So you took the whole entourage down to Miami . . .

Jules

Right?

Pharus

You were going down; might as well take the whole crew.

Loni

Ain't no fun if the homies can't have none.

Pharus

See that's . . . that's what I am talking about, y'all real loyal and hang together. How long you known Jules, Loni?

Loni

Shit, me and Jules go back to 8th Grade.

Jules

Oh yeah man, we . . .

Loni

I stopped these 9th Graders from smashing his face in.

Jules

Uh, save some of that . . .

Loni

Just saying, Ju', we close.

Pharus

And I can't lie. I'm jealous of that . . . You've seen all
my friends. Mostly older and white. No one I grew
up with. I love what y'all got. I'm jealous of that
tightness . . . Y'all were supposed to go down to
Miami, I showed up to the studio, you know, hoping
you would see me and be like . . . you know, 'Yo,
Pharus you can go too.' I mean, that would have made
my day . . . I was never picked as a kid.

Loni

Never?

Pharus

Nah. I was a li'l fat, you know, a li'l weaker than the
rest.

Loni

I had a weight problem, too.

Jules

Loni!

Loni

And Jules used to have buck teeth.

Pharus

So you understand me, then? You see what I'm saying.
I showed up when you were supposed to head out,

hoping I could tag along. To be a part of something. And I got to that studio and y'all was gone already . . . I broke down a li'l bit.

Loni and Jules
Yeah?

Pharus
That lonely, left-out feeling, it just hit me hard and I was riding the elevator down when I saw . . . I saw the exec, CEO . . . your boss. And he was mad nice, man. He took me to lunch, asked me if I was okay. I talked to him. Mostly about you. Man, I'm so sorry, Jules, Loni – I never wanted that to turn into . . . I never knew he would . . . You must think me such a punk.

Jules
Now he's crying.

Loni
Please don't . . . don't –

Jules
Loni, go get the man some tissue.

Loni
Yeah, Jules. Pharus?
Tissue.

Pharus
Back. Back, in the back.

Loni exits.

Jules
That was a nice story for Loni, man. You're good.

Pharus
I try.

Jules
Try harder. See, I know why that old man, rich old man, was looking for you. I know why he came

downstairs. I mean, he didn't risk getting questioned, asked, wondering what he was doing there, to see if he spotted a nice young man he took to lunch. Unless more than food was on the menu.

Pharus
I'm good company, Jules.

Jules
You funny, man.

Pharus
Thanks.

Jules
No, nigga, you *funny*. You like letting rich men touch you.

Pharus
I like it if they want me to.

Jules
If they pay you too.

Pharus
Damn, man, you caught on. See, I wanted to tell you.

Jules
No need. I got something you can be a part of.
It's my turn.

Pharus
I think we're better off friends, Jules.

Jules
No, *fuck* that.
This the deal, okay, I like to play a li'l game.

Pharus
GRAB.

Jules grabs Pharus from behind.

14

Jules

It's easy.
We just keep playing till you can't take no more.

Pharus

Jules –

Jules

Or . . . see, if I called the police, if I made enough noise
that the funders of this nice apartment, that sweet car,
get spooked and stop calling you for appointments –

Pharus

CARESS.

Jules

Don't worry, Pharus. I will make sure you stay well
paid, well fed. I'm a businessman. Not no faggot.
I wanna fuck you, not love you. But you can't blame
me for wanting you to be exclusively mine.

Loni enters.

Loni

Everything alright in here?

Jules

Yeah, this fool . . . this fool apologised. It's all good.
I stopped his crying for now.

Loni

We out, Jules?

Jules

We done for the day. Night.

Loni

Night.

Loni and Jules exit. Pharus sighs a deep, deep breath.

A Skype-type ring is heard. Pharus walks upstage.

Aunt Marian
Hiya!

Pharus
Hey.

Aunt Marian
Hiya is much nicer.

Pharus
Really?

Aunt Marian
I instruct all reception at Move –

Pharus
Move?

Aunt Marian
Yes, the PR firm that I run here in London.

Pharus
You're chatting me from London?
How did you get my –?

Aunt Marian
Pharus, dear, you've got to stop interrupting me.
You see, I know it's frustrating and all,
But I'm older and English. Means
We're allowed more time and space to speak.
Just the way it is.

Pharus
I apologise.

Aunt Marian
I'm your aunt.

Pharus
Oh. By divine right?

Aunt Marian

Ooh, I like that . . . attitude.
Boy, aren't you handsome standing there
In your skivvies.

She takes a sip.

Pharus

Are you drinking?

Aunt Marian

It's seven a.m. here, of course I am. How else'd you
expect th' day to get rolling?
I'm your Aunt Marian:
Your father's mother's sister. So that makes me your
great aunt.

Pharus

I never knew my father.

Aunt Marian

Right, he said that. And that's a shame
Because you never will.

Pharus

What?

Aunt Marian

He's dead.

Pharus

Oh, wow . . . You . . . Thanks.

Aunt Marian

Well, there's no need in sugar-coating . . . You can't
grieve a man you didn't know.
You should have more sympathy for me; I had to put
up with him.

Pharus

How'd he die?

Aunt Marian
Oh, peacefully in his sleep.

Pharus
Well, he's been dead to me. I'm sorry, don't mean to be rude but . . .

Aunt Marian
Hey! What's the matter with you? I told you not to interrupt –
You interrupt. I tell you I'm your aunt; you shrug it off. I say your father's dead; you turn on your heels to leave. You're pretty self-centred, aren't you?

Pharus
I'm not . . . I'm in some trouble.

Aunt Marian
What sort of trouble?

Pharus
Some shady, 'need-a-change-of-career' trouble.

Aunt Marian
Huh?
I told you I run a PR firm. Well, I run *the* PR firm.

Pharus
How you mean?

Aunt Marian
Well, I don't like to brag.

Pharus
I'm sensing that's a lie.

Aunt Marian
But you know Idi Amin?

Pharus
Heard of 'im.

Aunt Marian

Well, you would have heard a lot worse if we hadn't
got hold of him.

Pharus

Huh.

Aunt Marian

But that's all behind us now. We mostly work with
artists, celebrities of that nature.
No more cleaning up genocide. Just vomit from drunk
and disorderlies.
Equally as profitable yet somehow just as dangerous.
And
I've had the most remarkable idea: I want to start a
modelling wing here
At Move. Boy, with your charm and quick thinking,
You should work for me. What do you do there again?

Pharus

More like whom do I do here.

Aunt Marian

Say? I am sure you won't meet the clientele of our
calibre there. Whatever it is. High end, famous,
wealthy people who will turn to you to keep their
secrets.

Pharus

DING DING DING!

Aunt Marian

Come on, cocksucker, it will be fun! It's nepotism at its
best. Sorry for the language. (*Sips.*)

Pharus

Well, you can fill me in . . . when I get there!

Aunt Marian

So you'll do it! Yes! Lovely! Perfect!

You'll be working in direct opposition of my daughter,
your cousin, Val.
Hope that is alright.

Pharus

All the better. I've been known to be a kissing cousin.

Aunt Marian

When can we expect you?

Pharus

Have the car meet me . . . week's end? I have some
ends to tie up.

Aunt Marian

Until then. And Pharus . . .

Pharus

Ma'am.

Aunt Marian

Pack light.

Call ends. Lights out on Aunt Marian.

*There is a loud banging at the door. Pharus ducks and
hides, thinking it's the return of Jules and Loni. Then the
turning of keys. Girl Wonder enters. Pharus pops out,
scaring her.*

Girl Wonder

Hey, what the fuck, boy!

Pharus

Hey, Chante, sweet dear friend, thank th' Lord
It's you.

Girl Wonder

You scared me . . . Lord!

Pharus

I'm sorry. Where'd you just come from?

Girl Wonder
Work. I'm on my break –

Pharus
Perfect.
Help me.

Girl Wonder
Why is that always so easy for you to say?

Pharus
I help you.

Girl Wonder
Only when it fits you.

Pharus
Girl, this is a business transaction.
Now, do you know if Jules Mac Mana is in VIP tonight?

Girl Wonder
I haven't checked the list but they keep playing his
sexist ass
Music. Every other line calling us a bitch or a ho 'n
shit. I assume he'll be there.

Pharus
When Jules comes in I need you to seduce him.

Girl Wonder
What?

Pharus
Yeah, just get all up on him.
He's gotta play the part. Trust me.

Girl Wonder
I don't even like hip-hop.

Pharus
Neither does he really. But he's a loose end I need
To tie up. Do this, for me.

Girl Wonder

And for me? Can I get something I really want this time?

Pharus

No. But I will say this . . . I need a house-sitter –

Girl Wonder

Yeah, where are you going?

Pharus

Put it this way, we'll get the lease put in your name. Meantime!

Music spins, lights shift, and in comes Girl Wonder, letting us know we are in an exclusive sexy club. Jules comes into the club with his entourage. They post up in the VIP section. Girl Wonder wanders up to Jules.

Girl Wonder

Damn, Daddy, how you doing?

Loni

Eh, girl, that's Mr Daddy to you.

Girl Wonder

Get outta my face you two-bit side show.
I was talking to the man.

Entourage

DAMN!

Girl Wonder

Let me treat you to a private dance. As rough as you wanna be.

Jules

Sure, you do a private dance for me. But
Um . . . all my homies gotta watch.

Girl Wonder
Of course, Mr Daddy. Whatever you say.

*The Stage erupts. Music thumps on and we watch Girl
Wonder begin to give the boys, in the back, a dance to
remember. We shift focus.*

Enter Pharus with Senator Atwater.

Senator Atwater
Pharus! Pharus, slow down! I don't know why
You dragged me out of bed at this hour. And to . . .
To this part of town. I mean, I could be seen.

Pharus
Senator, that's sort of the point.

Senator Atwater
Listen, Pharus, I know I still owe you for not
Coming forth about . . . about that escapade you had
With my son –

Pharus
And your wife.

Senator Atwater
She, I care less about.

Pharus
She wanted it, sir.

Senator Atwater
I recognise, but if we gave women what they wanted
we wouldn't be men.
Listen, son, I won't be blackmailed.
Huh. that's funny 'cause you are a, you know . . . a
black male.

Pharus
Technically: mixed race.

Senator Atwater

Only while Obama's in office. After that
You'll go back to being black. Trust me.

Pharus

Touché. But that's exactly why I have brought you
Here. I actually want to help you.

Senator Atwater

Go on.

Pharus

Election time coming up and you keep getting painted
as the hard
Nose old school out of touch . . .

Senator Atwater

Get to the point, son, I could have stayed in bed with
the wife to hear
That kind of . . .

Pharus

What if you get seen in a nightclub trying to reach out,
trying to
Talk to the people about the issues that concern them
and are met with
Hostility. What if you made a point to seek out the
hip-hop moguls on their
Terms and talk to them about the violence and
defamation of women in their
Music and . . .

Senator Atwater

And they don't want to hear it!

Pharus

Then, you look like the victim.

Senator Atwater

But I'm just trying to reach out and save the urban
youth from the violence

That tears at our community, ha-ah! That's good.
You sure you don't wanna
Work for me?

Pharus

I already have, your son paid me from your account.
Now remember you're just here to hear people out and
find a way to instil core American values back into the
cities and suburbs of America.

Senator Atwater

You sure it'll be met with hostility?

Pharus

American core values incite hostility the world over.

*Jules has spotted Pharus. He is on him like white on
rice.*

Just the man I wanted to see.

Jules

You ready to do what I asked you to?

Pharus

I'm thinking about it, meantime I need to introduce you
To someone.

Girl Wonder (*coming in to Jules*)

Hey, Boo!

Senator Atwater

Got your honeys, I see.

Girl Wonder (*hugging Jules*)

That's right!

Jules

Girl, get off me. Who's this?

Pharus

Jules, gang, this is one of my *friends* – Senator Atwater.

Senator Atwater

Nice of you to allow me to talk to you,
Young man. I need a high profile in touch with the urban
Youth, person like yourself, to help put me back in direct contact
With the people. You know what I'm saying?

Jules

Not really.

Senator Atwater

Well, here this must be your pretty li'l . . .

Girl Wonder

Soon-to-be wifey!

Jules

What!

Senator Atwater

Your fiancée'? Great!
See, you believe in strong family values. But sometimes your music doesn't reflect . . .

Jules

Man, this bitch ain't my wife!

Loni

We don't love them hoes!

Jules

I ain't married to this or no girl.

Senator Atwater

Well, how do you feel about gay marriage?

Loni

Yo, Jules, you gone let this old man punk you like that?

Girl Wonder

Oh hell, nah, no man of mine gone be supporting
Those Whitney-singing friends of Dorothy's.

Jules

Eh girl, shut the fuck up!

Loni

Nothing wrong with a li'l Whitney, though.

Jules

Loni!

Senator Atwater

Wow, I am really glad.
Pharus told me to come down here to get a great idea
About what the community needs and doesn't and
Our little chat has helped tremendously. Thanks, you
the man.

Pharus takes a photo of them.

Pharus

Say 'aah'!

*Flash. The stage whites out. Music blares. We catch up
to Sherman Kanderebitz, dancing to the music as he
broadcasts his v-log.*

Sherman Kanderebitz

WHAT UP YO!
I'm your man Sherman Kanderebitz with this
Breaking news from the street. Remember you
Heard it first here on WHAT UP YO! News!
The hip-hop industry is being sucker punched
And this time it's getting into the political arena with
A champion. Senator Atwater, Republican of New
York, has vowed
To open a congressional hearing that will call into
Question hip-hop's direct effect on the community.
Check him out.

Senator Atwater

I'm a Christian man. And though some things that go
on in people's private

Lives I may not agree with, I don't go around writing
songs boasting
That I hate them, will burn them, gun them down if
I catch them in my cul-de-sac!
So we're gonna call these hip-hop artists and CEO's
into question. Get them to face the mothers, sisters,
and brothers they offend. And it's not just this white
old man trying to win re-election. Listen up, I've got a
strong wall of mothers, churchgoing Dr King
Marching people behind this Republican ready to take
on . . .
The sad thing is I tried reaching out to that uh . . . uh,
Jules Mac Mana. I met with
Him at one of his clubs. I wanted to reason and talk
about the effect his music had on youth. He was drunk,
belligerent and he had his, I think, pregnant fiancée
dancing
Around a pole for a whole group of guys calling her
names in public. What kind of role model is that?

Sherman Kanderebitz

Whoa! He called Young Jules out, son!
Needless to say Jules and his sideman
Loni Fromray won't be appearing at any concerts,
Or clubs for that matter, since Ditch Diggin' Records'
Parent company has suspended any public appearances
until after this congressional
Hearing or bad press firestorm dies. And speaking of
bad press.
WHAT UP YO! signs off with its weirdest clip of
November. We move from the
Gridlock US government to the streets of London with
The interview from coming-of-age star Sylvia Watson.
Have you seen this? It's pitiful. All we have to
Say Sylvia is WHAT UP YO!

Shift. Lights come up on Sylvia Watson trying to escape the pap and interviewer. She looks terrified.

Interviewer

Do you like your fans?

Sylvia

I try not to talk to them.

Interviewer

Are you admitting that you avoid fans?

Sylvia

I'm . . . I'm shy . . . really, and I keep trying to explain that to people,
But they . . . they . . .

Interviewer

So you don't appreciate your fans?

Sylvia

I do . . . I just wish they could see
Me for more than a magic sidekick of some androgynous
Wizard.

Press

Do the bumble?

Interviewer

What . . . what should they see you as?

Sylvia

A bloody person. I mean, how many *Punch and the Magic Bee* movies
Do you think we could make? I heard my voice on the playback and thought, oh God, who is that? I sound like a dick. I've been doing it to sound like the character, a dick.

Interviewer

Aw, can you do the bee again?

Sylvia

I'm not the fucking bee! Stop pointing that. How
Would you like it? If I stuck that in your face?

Interviewer

Well, I'm not a star.

Sylvia

Well, if it were up to me I wouldn't be either!

Act Two

Lights shift and Sylvia is sitting in the office of Move.
Sam Qwik holds an iPad and Val works the meeting.

Valentina
Sylvia!
Who, what, when, where?
Why, why, why? Why did you say that on camera,
Sylvia?

Sylvia
Well, I was waiting . . .

Valentina
I asked you to wait, I know I did.
I said wait. The filming is done,
Wait. Go on holiday, visit family.
Do not, whatever you do, do not give any press.

Qwik
Won't have to worry about that now.

Valentina
Qwik!

Qwik
After that awful clip. It just went viral.

Valentina
It wasn't awful, it was . . .

Qwik
Damaging.

Valentina
I was going to say . . .

Qwik
Career-destroying.

Valentina
If you are not quiet, Sam Qwik, your option to create
Children without the use of a straw will be
Severely limited.
Sylvia, this is the reason why I asked, advised you
As your press agent, your publicist. I'm almost your
Manager . . . I gave you that advice as a, a sister.

Sylvia
Look, it just happened. We finished the last film,
I was leaving set and
Everyone kept asking what I was doing next. And
people
Were like, 'You got less annoying as the series went on.'
What's next? I just wanted to say, 'I don't know.
I don't know and
If I did, I wouldn't fucking tell you if I did . . .'

Cries and pops a pill.

Valentina
Don't cry. What's that you're popping?

Sylvia
Xanax, Zoloft.

Shrugs.

Val, I've fucked everything up.

Valentina
Look, you have a fan base, Sylvia, you just
Have to be careful where you lead them;
Go home. Get some rest, we will figure out a strategic
And awe-inspiring plan to right this wrong.

Sylvia
Promise?

Valentina

I do.

Sylvia exits. Val tries to throttle Qwik.

Valentina

What, were you trying to get Sylvia to walk from us?

Qwik

Be nice to have that disaster off our books, don't
You think? I was being pro-active.

Valentina

This is not how this campaign is supposed to go.
I mean, we knew she was a socially awkward, that's why
We protected her. She's still just a kid. She does have a
great deal of promise. She can act. She can sing . . .
Fuck. We have to make sure my mother doesn't find
out about this.

Enter Aunt Marian with Sylvia.

Aunt Marian

All of London is talking about it!
The most amazing part about th' absurdity
Was you had the best intentions. I could see it in your
Face. Didn't mean any harm, of course.

Sylvia

I was just saying that I was uncomfortable, that
There's more to me than just a kid on a film.

Aunt Marian

Oh sorry, so sorry, my dear child star, so sorry you
Did not enjoy your sidekick role as a poof's magic
Imaginary friend.

Qwik

Whoa!

Aunt Marian

But you were cast out of that dark

Dark obscurity you now long for, into the spotlight.
And once that filthy dingy light has landed in your pores
There is no wash-away. It's photosynthesis.

Valentina
Mother!

Sylvia
What are you saying?

Aunt Marian
I'm sick of these talents with their bizarre oddities
Who yearn, demand, spit down your throat
To get them attention, get them the job,
Liven their profile, and then right after the sun
Becomes too harsh . . .

Sylvia
Please!

Aunt Marian
They are backing away.

Sylvia
I'm not . . .

Aunt Marian
Begging you to shield them from its rays.
I say get darker like the Saracen,
Learn to live with sunspots.
Adjust, adapt, evolve, you cowards.

Valentina
Mother, stop!

Aunt Marian
Why should I? All that I built in this company
Is heading down the drain with this one.

Sylvia
How?

Aunt Marian

How? You think anyone out there, the people who
We honestly represent, are gonna let us get away
Letting one of our star clients melt down all over the
Telly? No one's going to trust us, or come to us, or . . .
Well, what should we do?

Qwik

I feel like we should lighten the load.

Aunt Marian

Amen.

Sylvia starts crying, pops a pill.

Valentina

Calm down, slow down. Listen to me. What we will
do . . . What I will
Do, is personally handle this situation. Sylvia and
Myself will come up with a way to spin this.

Aunt Marian

Oh good.

Valentina

Mother, don't fight me on –
What?

Aunt Marian (*loudly*)

I think it's a wonderful idea! Wonderful! And meantime
I personally will focus on the launch of the Models at
Move.

Stands.

Valentina

The what?

Aunt Marian

Yes, it's a new initiative. I've always wanted to. And
now
That you are tackling the PR sector, I can focus on this
endeavour.

Valentina
Mother that will take . . . I mean you would have to
hire –

Aunt Marian
I already have.
Don't worry, he's family, you can trust him.

Valentina
Who?

Aunt Marian
Pharus. His name his Pharus.

Valentina
Charlie's boy?

Aunt Marian
Charlie's boy from America.

Qwik
He arrives from the airport this evening.

Valentina (*to Qwik*)
You knew!

Aunt Marian
Qwik!
You call the board and some press, get a bumping
DJ and we will throw Pharus a wonderful welcome
announcement
Party! Won't that be fun?

Valentina
Mother, wait . . .

Aunt Marian
No time, dear, gotta make some calls. Qwik, come
Help me with the Skype. You'd better get on with
whatever
It is you're going to do with Sylvia, dear. If this fails,

36

I will
Have to shut Move PR down permanently.

*We hear the roar of an airplane. Lights bump and we
find Pharus seated in Business Class next to Snooty Lady
who is waking up. She has a blanket over her lap. Girl
Wonder appears, dressed like a flight attendant. She
makes an announcement.*

Girl Wonder
Good evening, passengers, I'm sure it's been a difficult
life for some of you, you see the captain has turned on
the 'Fasten Seat Belt' signs indicating that we are on
our initial descent into the Heathrow Airport area.
And even though we foretold of this happening and
asked that you comply and hop to your seats I still see
quite a lot of you roaming around, navel-gazing,
conversing, and gallivanting. Please discontinue use of
all electronic devices, particularly mobile phones, put
them away, forever, don't just check the time or the
weather or . . . Throw them into the nadir of your
wasteland hand luggage and keep them there until you
are out of the customs area, past border patrol, and on
route to your final destination. Thank you. Flight
attendants, prepare for arrival.

Pharus (*with phone in his hand*)
It's so funny they act like the world would
Come to an end if one cell phone is . . .

*Snooty Lady presses the call button. Girl Wonder
appears.*

Girl Wonder
Yes?

Snooty Lady
This one has his mobile phone on.

Pharus
I do . . . what?

Girl Wonder
Oh, we have one of those, do we?

Snooty Lady
Yes . . .

Pharus
One of . . . *Chante?*

Girl Wonder
Oh, do you speak French? *Parlez-vous français?*

Pharus
No . . . No, you look just like . . .

Girl Wonder
That's lovely, dear, I don't care for your sweet American
Charm that might have worked a few marks back past
th' Prime Meridian but your cute face and Obama
curls won't
Do anything for me, sir. Besides the minute I fall for it
you'd
Just up and leave me for some white girl.

Pharus
White what?

Girl Wonder
Your device, sir!

Pharus
I'm trying. It's on airplane mode, it takes a minute.
There, see? Done.

Girl Wonder
Please comply with all safety regulations. Don't make
me come back here.

She exits.

Pharus
Why didn't you just ask me to?

Snooty Lady
They had already.

Pharus
Listen, you've been humming and hahing
The whole ride. I don't even know you, lady.

Snooty Lady
And yet it doesn't seem to stop you speaking.

Pharus
I was trying to brighten your day.

Snooty Lady
They've installed these handy lights for that, so you
can save the lip service.

Pharus
Oh man, why you hate me?

Snooty Lady
I don't . . . hate you . . .

Pharus
C'mon, you're just being evil, and you saw I was
Trying to turn off this phone, you didn't have to
Call the flight attendant over.

Snooty Lady
You weren't listening . . .

Pharus
How do you know?

Snooty Lady
Because you people never do.

Pharus
'You people'!

Snooty Lady

You never take into consideration the fears of others
Whether others get nervous or terrified on flights and
you gadget-people
Just keep right on with your apps and your fingering,
you won't
Learn until you bring a carrier down!

Pharus

Yo . . . Yo . . . chill, shhh!

Snooty Lady

I'm . . . sorry.

Pharus

Don't be. You gotta stay calm.

Snooty Lady

I'm trying!

Pharus

Well, what do you normally do?

Snooty Lady

Panic.

Pharus

Okay, well we can't have that – let me help.

Snooty Lady

Are you a therapist?

Pharus

Kinda . . .
I'm coming out of retirement.
Just breathe.

Snooty Lady

Alright.

Pharus

Close your eyes.

Snooty Lady

Fine.

Pharus, gently, reaches under her blanket.

Oh –
Excuse me! What are you doing?

Pharus

The only therapy I know. Feeling better?

Snooty Lady

I – Yes. You . . . people will see!

Pharus

It's Business Class, everyone minds their own.

Snooty Lady

What if someone moves to go to the toilet?

Pharus

Well, you'll just have to keep lookout . . .

Snooty Lady

I . . . where are you? What are you doing?

Pharus

More lip service.

Pharus goes under her blanket and begins to perform cunnilingus. He is completely covered by the blanket. Girl Wonder comes back, calling.

Girl Wonder

Seat belts,
Seat belts,
Seat . . .
Where's the gentleman who was . . .

Snooty Lady

I . . . He . . . Oooh . . .

Girl Wonder

Say again, love?

Snooty Lady
Toilet.

Girl Wonder
The 'Fasten Your Seat Belt' sign is on.

Snooty Lady
Mmm.

Girl Wonder
I need you to buckle –

Snooty Lady
– up!

Girl Wonder
Yes, we'll be –

Snooty Lady
– there in a moment!

Girl Wonder exits. Pharus pops his head up.

Pharus
Good work.

Snooty Lady (*pushing him back under*)
Go to work.
Ooh . . .
Ah!

Girl Wonder (*off*)
Flight attendants, please prepare for landing.

The roar of the plane landing is timed with Snooty Lady's climax.

Snooty Lady
YES!

Plane sounds die. Pharus emerges.

Pharus

See, I got you on the ground.

Snooty Lady (*hitting him*)

You stupid . . . stupid!

Pharus

What, what, what? Look, I helped you
With your fear of flying the best I knew how.

Snooty Lady (*flushed*)

God . . . I mean, thanks. But
This was . . . no, but you are not
Something I want to be involved with.

Pharus

Back to hating me.

Snooty Lady

I don't hate you, you're just . . .

Pharus

What would you rather?

Snooty Lady

Someone a little less oily and diplomatic.

Pharus

Ah, like your husband?

Snooty Lady

How did you . . .?

Pharus

Don't be shy, it's my job to catch these things. What's
he, a politician?

Snooty Lady

Ambassador. This job of yours must be pretty amazing.

Pharus

Huh. I don't normally do this but
Let me take down your number?

Snooty Lady
   For . . .

Pharus
   Just in case I find someone else who speaks
   In tongues.

Snooty Lady
   I – no . . .

Pharus (*taking out phone*)
   Come on.

Snooty Lady
   Well, don't turn that on.
   Look, here's my card.

Pharus
   Well, it's easier to . . .

Girl Wonder (*reappearing*)
   Sir, is that cell phone on again?

   Lights.

Office at Move.

Valentina
   Unfortunately.
   You are the only one who can do this next thing
   For me.

Qwik
   I'm not into dressing up like a woman.

Valentina
   What?

Qwik
   When are you going to tell Mummy that you're
   A muff-diver!

Valentina

I beg your pardon . . .

Lord Fairway enters.

Oh, hello, Lord Fairway.

Qwik

My Lord . . .

Valentina

We were just . . .

Lord Fairway

Carry on, carry on, didn't hear anything about muffs
and diving. Carry on.

He exits.

Valentina

What is going on here?

Qwik

We're starting a party.

Valentina

For some cousin who isn't here yet, but is about to be
made head of
A part of our company, my company, that doesn't exist!
While my mother, your boss, is dampening her
neurological
Make-up at every turn with firewater and making
irrational
Decisions so she can pretend to be Tyra Banks!
G'LORD! I can't
Freak out . . . I've gotta stay calm, this all can work.
I can't think about this party now, I have to focus.
I'm a clear-thinking individual who, regardless of her
upbringing, can overcome, and I deserve, like all
creatures, peace. I love my job. I love my job, I love
my clients. Especially those like Sylvia Watson.

Qwik

How's that head doctor working out?

Valentina

You have all the accounts in your desk.
Get in the system, call up the bank, move some funds over to this account.

She hands him a slip.

There is a service apartment near, set up a month's stay for two.
Please follow my instructions exactly.

Qwik

Does this have anything to do with that
Pounds to dollars transfer you made earlier?

Valentina

How did you . . . ? Jesus, did you tap my phone?

Qwik

No, this isn't *The Bill*, darling, I just pick up my end and listen.

Valentina (*sighs*)

I need you to send a car to the airport. Call the car company, tell them to send the driver,
The girl we . . . we normally use. I need her, she's reliable, to pick up some very important people.
Please.

Qwik

Is Pharus one of them?

Valentina

Who? Pharus? Oh no . . . Good God, no. I don't care if he
Ever shows up. I'm not quite sure if he's not some figment

Of Drunkzilla's imagination.
Car, quietly! This is important.

Qwik
Who should I have the driver wait for?

Valentina
Have her hold a sign that says 'MOVE'.
They'll come to her.

Qwik
This better not be to get some mail-order bride you sent
Over. Enough moody women round here.

Sylvia enters.

Sylvia
Val.

Valentina
Sylvia.

Sylvia
Shh, is anyone listening?

Valentina
No, I don't . . . No. I thought you were home.

Sylvia
I was . . . but all the way the driver was staring at
Me and I just . . . I was afraid to call in case they had
tapped my phone.
And then all this email and Twitter, little kids everywhere
Hate me. And teenagers calling me
Things. I just . . .

She pops a pill.

Valentina
Wait, Sylvia, it will pass. You need to rest – you don't
look so good.

Sylvia

Wait, is someone listening? I . . . I gotta go . . . I gotta get away.

She backs out of the room.

Valentina

What do you mean? Sylvia? Sylvia!

Act Three

An interview room at Border Patrol. Pharus is in a chair next to Ragiv.

Ragiv

Welcome to Border Patrol!

Pharus

What . . . what the hell just happened?

Ragiv

Hello. Pharus, right?

Pharus

We know each other?

Ragiv

Seems we missed each other on the way
Up, boss.

Pharus

I don't follow.

Ragiv

Oh, it must be the transatlantic jet leg. Happens to the best of us.
Even my brain was a little jangled when I first got here. I handed them my passport
Which to them looked a little fishy. Well, of course I dummied
Up while they took the piss asking where I was from, why
I was here, what was my purpose . . . You know, all the existentials.
And then one of the patrol rushed in, said there was a problem aboard

A flight from JFK. Seems a moody flight attendant
confiscated –

Holds up Pharus's phone.

A brand new mobile from a rude passenger and they
were bringing
Him here for questioning.

Pharus
Son of a –

Ragiv
Bitch, I know! No sense of privacy these . . . leaving a
man's personal device
Sitting around like that. Lucky I grabbed it for you,
boss!

Pharus
Okay, you need to stop calling me that.
You stole this.

Ragiv
'S not what I told them. No, right, when they started
Talking about a removal centre for me and the nights
on that
Cold concrete came back to me, it all flooded, my
memory.
Yup, you being my boss, seeing me, hiring me to be
one of your next top
Models and bringing me to the UK to start a new life
at – what's it called? 'Move'.

Pharus
Wow, that's nice, man, real nice. I'm impressed.
Listen, if you knew what I really did –

Ragiv
I know it ain't running a modelling agency. Some of
these texts

Are racy, man. 'Can I lick what I like?' Reply 'Always.
Standard Price.'

Pharus

What do you want?

Ragiv

Out of here.

Pharus

I can't do that.

Ragiv

Why not? You seem to be able to do a lot. Do this.
You hired me, and are helping me process my
Visa straight way.

Pharus

Ha! No, look, sorry, I'm gonna tell these guys the
truth.

Ragiv

I already did. Howsit that you don't get
That? I already told them the truth as
Far as you and I can know it.

Pharus

Yo, I can't hire you! I'm here to work for my aunt.
I don't know you.
Far as I know you're –

Ragiv

A terrorist plot?

Pharus

Maybe.

Ragiv

And you're the American ringleader?

Pharus

What?

Ragiv

I'm just saying! Whichever way you want to go,
Boss, I'm with you. We can be models in the
Fashion world or a threat to homeland security.
Whatever it is, I'm with you. You're my guy.

Pharus

Fuck! Wow! Fuck!

Ragiv

Look,
They come in, we tell them our
Tale and . . . freedom. In fact you never have to see me
again.

Officer Percy and Officer Jeff Thibodeux enter.

Officer Percy

Alright, let's see that passport, lad.

Pharus

I'm sorry –

Officer Jeff Thibodeux

Get out your passport.

Pharus

Okay, no problem.
(*To Ragiv.*) Let me lead.

Ragiv

Your dance.

Officer Jeff Thibodeux

You're lucky we got you here, 'stead of
Just sending you back to the USA. What
You were doing was a criminal offence.

Officer Percy

Even if it was bloody funny. I mean, did
You see that stewardess's face when . . .

Officer Jeff Thibodeux clears his throat.

You've got to follow the rules here. If your client
hadn't said when
He did, you'd be in hot water.

Pharus
He's a good man.

Officer Jeff Thibodeux
We got a call from your agency, seems
It's pretty well-connected. Needed to check your
Whereabouts, said they'd rushed your papers ahead.

Pharus
Kind of them.

Officer Jeff Thibodeux
Seems they have no papers on him (*Ragiv*), though.
(*To Ragiv.*) What's it called again?

Pharus
'Move Ltd'.

Officer Jeff Thibodeux
I asked *him*.

Pharus
I've asked him not to speak.

Both Officers
Why?

Officer Jeff Thibodeux
He can't speak for himself?

Pharus
Well, that's my job as his agent, to speak
For him.
Course he can speak, speak.

Ragiv
'Move Ltd'.

Pharus
See.

Officer Jeff Thibodeux
Who runs it?

Ragiv
He does.

Pharus
He's, he's, he's over-zealous and too kind.
Stupid kid.
Marian Stephenson runs it.

Officer Jeff Thibodeux
And when was Move Ltd established?

Ragiv
Pre-colonial times.

Pharus
Ha!

Officer Jeff Thibodeux (*to Pharus*)
Shut up.
What's his name?

Pharus looks to Ragiv, who is unseen by the officers.
Ragiv tries to mouth-motion his name to Pharus.

Pharus
Ra-giv . . . Well his stage name is Ragiv.

Officer Percy (*looking at passport*)
Ragiv.
Says just Ragiv.

Officer Jeff Thibodeux
Just checking.

Pharus
For what?

Officer Percy
He's making sure you are who you say
You are. I told him, who would want to
Pretend to be a talent agent? Those guys
Are scum. No offence.

Pharus
None taken.
Would you like me to be something else?

Officer Jeff Thibodeux
Long as you're not a terrorist. I'm going to go
Call Move and speak to Marian Stephenson.

Pharus
Send her my love.

Officer Jeff Thibodeux exits.

You've got to help us.

Officer Percy
I do?

Ragiv
He does?

Pharus
He's our only hope.

Officer Percy
Only hope?

Pharus
I don't think your fellow officer takes his station as
serious as you.

Officer Percy
Oh, Jeff? No, he's pretty serious

Pharus
About protecting

The borders and welcoming the poor defenceless,
And embattled?

Officer Percy
Is that what we do?

Pharus
Every day. And here, this man Ragiv,
Originally he's from a place, whose very name if
I even mention it he starts to get the shivers –

Officer Percy
Where?

Pharus
One clue. 'We jammin!'

Officer Percy
Jamaica?

Playing along, Ragiv doubles over.

Ragiv
Uh –

Pharus (*to Officer Percy*)
Shhh!

Officer Percy
He doesn't look Jamaican.

Pharus
He's Chinese Jamaican.

Ragiv
Yeah, mon.

Pharus
See? And he asked me not to tell you.
And I promised I wouldn't. He didn't want to elicit
your pity.

Ragiv

Don't want no pity, mon!

Pharus

But Ragiv, this man has a heart, let him hear you.

Officer Percy

What's wrong with him?

Pharus

Wrong! Nothing's wrong with him, 'Baby, he was born this way.'

Officer Percy

Wha . . . Born this . . .

Becoming clear.

Oh.

Pharus

Oh yes. You see, when he was a little Chinese Jamaican growing up in the foothills of the Blue Mountains, all the boys would chase him calling him Terrible names.

Ragiv

Batty man!

Pharus

Chase him with sticks and sometimes machetes.

Ragiv

Chi-chi man.

Officer Percy

My God.

Pharus

But see, I found him and I thought . . . oh my, this is the most beautiful man I've ever seen, I want to do photo shoots and show the world what the mixture of The old world and the new can make.

Officer Percy
Old world?

Pharus
But the Jamaican government wouldn't have a chi-chi
man being on billboards, so we came here.

Ragiv
Mi so tired of running.

Pharus
I am too, Ragiv, but this may be where we stop.
Here we can love freely.

Officer Percy
What?

Pharus
Oh, I've said it!

Ragiv
You shouldn't say!

Pharus
But I have.

Ragiv
But that doesn't make me a gay, mon.

Pharus
No, no, it just means you love me,
And you see that's why we can't tell my aunt.
Because she won't let him come over if he
Works for me and we're in love, but it's the only
Way to save him from an uncertain life and the
Pain of being so far away. Oh, Ragiv!

Ragiv
Oh, Pharus!

Officer Percy
I wish I could help.

Pharus
You can.

Officer Percy
I can?

Pharus
Sure . . . right now you can make it alright for Ragiv,
For us. I mean you will see in a moment; I have a work
Visa in process and my papers are coming any moment.
But for Ragiv, all he needs is one Border Patrol to stamp
His passport with –

Ragiv
'Exceptional leave to remain'.

Pharus
'Exceptional leave to remain'. Sadly the UK won't grant
Sexual persecution asylum so easily, it's rarely done.
But if you see fit, sir, you can make our world aright.
What say you?

Ragiv
Oh, him laughing at we, now.

Officer Percy
No, I'm not.

Pharus
Sure you are. You think we're disgusting.

Officer Percy
Not true, my . . . brother, dances at th' other end of
the ballroom.

Pharus
Does he? Is he single?

Ragiv
Slut.

Pharus
I'm only kidding.

Ragiv
I know, it's just the stress, it's getting to me!

Pharus
It's breaking you!

Ragiv
It's destroying we!

Officer Percy
No! I won't let it.
Here . . .

He takes a stamp and stamps their passports.

Once, the boys took the ball from my . . . brother and no one helped him.

Pharus
But now you are. You are.
Thank you.

Ragiv
Thank you.

Officer Percy
Alright, fellas. Have . . . love.

Ragiv and Pharus exit.

Party. Offices at Move. Val interrupts the party.

Valentina
Ladies and gentlemen.
I am sorry to cut the festivities short.
Our dear Pharus is late, probably battling the
Elements as you all did to be here today.
But those of you who have to leave, I
Would not rest or get a moment's sleep if I didn't
Update you on something before you heard it on the
news. This very night.

Our dear Sylvia Watson, prized client, tried to take
Her own life.
She
Came here, staggering in speech, heartbroken; she
looked
Up with those innocent and shy eyes and said to me,
'Do not hate me, tell them not to hate me, if they
dislike
Me so much I will take myself away. I am not afraid.'
I must go now to be near my friend in her time of need.
Enjoy your soirée.

Back at Heathrow.

Ragiv
Son! That was nasty, you know, I ain't
Never seen nothing like it. You were
Fucking amazing.

Pharus
Thanks.

Ragiv
I mean that. I ain't just shining you
Up, pound. You're real gold, you are.

Pharus
I always thought myself a copper tone.

Ragiv
Funny, funny. So is that what you really do?

Pharus
Yeah man. I mean, I thought I would
Try something different, maybe an honest day's work.
But . . .

Ragiv
Tell me about it.

Pharus

Aren't you supposed to be kissing the
Ground thanking the crown for the blessings
Of liberty?

Ragiv

You know how many times I been over?

Pharus

Why'd you leave?

Ragiv

I got my reasons. But I'm here, thank you.

Pharus

I don't want your thanks.

Ragiv

Hey man, all that lovey-dovey was just an act.

Pharus

I don't want your love either, man.

Ragiv

Sure?

Pharus

I mean, to be honest, I can't force you to do anything.
I mean, I'll pay you. You impressed me. Not many can
Do that.

Ragiv

You're the one that saved the day.

Pharus

Yeah, but you got me to do it. I mean, you forced me
Basically. Made me have no choice but to help you.
Can use someone like you.

Ragiv

Use?

Pharus

You used me. Look, point being
You seem like a man of your words.
One of them was, you follow where I
Lead. This where I'm going, you coming?

Ragiv

I . . . I got something to take care of.

Pharus

Yeah, I figured.

Ragiv

Don't . . . I'm telling . . . I'm serious, man. I got
Something to take care of tonight but tomorrow I
Will meet you bright and early for a full
Briefing and that.

Pharus

Right.

Ragiv

Thanks, Pharus.

Pharus

Yeah.

*Ragiv exits. Red walks by holding up a 'Move Ltd'
sign.*

Oh . . . hey, what does your sign say?

Red

If you can't read it, darling, it's not for you.

Pharus

I work for Move, you here for me?

Red

Must be. They said you would come to me.

Pharus

Well, it was an inviting offer.

Red

I think you're sticking your rod in the wrong loch.

Pharus

What?

Red

Scottish expression.
They said there was two of you?

Officer Jeff Thibodeux enters.

Pharus

Two? Grab!

Officer Jeff grabs Pharus. Pharus turns to Red.

Wait!

Red exits.

Officer Jeff Thibodeux

I need to speak with you.

Pharus

I –

Officer Jeff Thibodeux

Percy shouldn't have let you go off like that.

Pharus

Well, we talked everything out, so don't worry –

Officer Jeff Thibodeux

I've been doing some checking on you.

Pharus

Hey, listen, I . . . I know I shouldn't have lapped the
woman on the plane but that was for free and I was
thinking some pretty bad things. But I promise you
I wasn't going back into my old ways. I came here for
a fresh shot. I just wanted to start a new life with this
new job.

Officer Jeff Thibodeux

Yeah, well, everyone deserves one of those. I just need to know you're not going to take advantage.

Pharus

Advantage?

Officer Jeff Thibodeux

Huh.

You ever wanted to be someone's fairy tale?

Pharus

I think I have been, but I don't think were talking the same –

Officer Jeff Thibodeux

They raided this shop somewhere in the East End and they found

A shit load of girls in the back. All illegals. And they

Were sending them back through here, on my watch. And

I was supposed to

Escort one back to her flight but on the way . . .

I couldn't. I just couldn't. 'Cause she said to me in broken English

She said to me, the only thing she ever wanted was a fairy tale. To be the princess.

Pharus

Wow, that's –

Officer Jeff Thibodeux

Broke my heart. I couldn't send her back.

But she can't stay if she's not legal. But you . . . you can change that.

Pharus

I don't see how I –

Officer Jeff Thibodeux

Here's her picture.

Pharus

She's . . . nice.

Officer Jeff Thibodeux

Nice! You don't think she's beautiful! I mean,
We've been poring over these magazines and
Practising. God we've been practising.

Pharus

I bet.

Officer Jeff Thibodeux

I'm telling you, she could do it. She's got
What it takes and once you meet her you'll melt.
And . . . and who cares if you don't . . .
You don't deserve
Your job anyway. Your aunt gave you that job, you
Don't even have the proper qualifications.

Pharus

The job! Yes, model agent, yeah!
Well, you don't need qualifications to be an agent. You
Sort of just wave your arms around and say
Darling a lot.

Officer Jeff Thibodeux

Well, that's in direct violation of the tier programme
which
Your visa falls under. I could send you back to the
States.
But I don't wanna do that. Because like you, there is
someone
Who needs an opportunity. Just . . . just give her a
chance. Please!

Pharus

Why don't you just *give* her a visa!

Officer Jeff Thibodeux

Because I believe in doing things by the book!

There's law and order. But we can't have her going
back to Prussia.

Pharus

Prussia isn't –

Officer Jeff Thibodeux

Maybe if this works out, she can stay and I could
introduce her to my mum.
Never knew anyone who loves me like this. Like I'm
under a spell. Doing things I wouldn't normally do.
You know that feeling?

Pharus

Yeah, I just learned it. Listen, here's my card. Just
show up tomorrow.

Officer Jeff Thibodeux

Thank you. Thank you, she'll be great. You'll see. See
you tomorrow.

Officer Jeff Thibodeux exits.

Pharus

Yeah, yeah, great,
Eh! How do I get to central London from here?

Girl Wonder appears.

Girl Wonder

Ladies and gentleman, the last Piccadilly Line train
calling
At all stops to central London –

She looks at her watch.

Has departed. If you desire to travel into central
London from
This time forward, there is a good bus service leaving
the Heathrow
Station . . . But I guarantee you, it will be the longest
and most complicated

Journey you've ever taken. Have a great evening and
thank you for trusting TFL. Oh and don't take rides
with, or in, unarranged unmarked taxis. It's illegal.

Pharus
Ain't this about a bitch!

Cabbie enters.

Cabbie
Need a lift? Where you going?

Pharus
Shhh!
I know that loud woman just said don't
Take rides in unarranged coaches but
Hear me, I just need to get to London.
I don't have much
Money on me but I swear, when we get to my aunt's
Office, she'll give all the money, plus twenty per cent
tip.

Cabbie
Nice aunt.

Pharus
I ain't even met her yet.

Cabbie
Trusting.

Pharus
At this point, man, I ain't got no choice!

Cabbie
Well, we all have a choice.

Pharus
I hope you choose to take my ass down to
The office.

Cabbie

Alright, you're American, right?

Pharus

What gave it away, the desperation or the accent?

Cabbie

The accent. We've got desperate here, too.

Pharus

Really?

Cabbie

Yeah, but we're just too polite to show it to you.

Pharus

That's kind, I think. You're kind, I think.

Cabbie

I'll take you, kiddo. Stop trying to sleep with me.

Pharus

Sorry, it just comes out. Professional courtesy.

Cabbie

Oh yeah, what do you do?

Pharus

Today? I feel like: UN peacekeeper.

Cabbie (*turns hot anger*)

Get the fuck away from me!

Pharus

What, why?

Cabbie

Fucking warmongers, all.

Pharus

Whoa!

Laughs.

Cabbie

You think it's funny to keep going round the world,
Acting like you're there for peace, acting like you have
Some say, stirring up these dickhead dictators only to
Realise you can't bloody well solve the problem in the
first!
So, who next do you call in? Who comes to sort out
the hive
You hit like a fucking *piñata*?

Pharus

Look, I'm sorry . . .

Cabbie

Fuck you! Are you sorry we can't sleep at night?
Are you sorry to those lads and girls down at the lines
watching friends blow up
Or carrying away the civilians who spit on you in
some foreign
Language you didn't have time to learn before you
were shipped?
Bet you don't jump out your bed when a car backfires,
or leave your
Sleep to find the floor 'cause the kids leave the fucking
telly on and some
Git BBC reporter decided to do live playback from the
front lines.

Pharus

I'm in entertainment, modelling.
I'm sorry, I should have said sooner.
Hey, you alright, man?

Cabbie

Oh . . . oh, sorry, mate.
I probably scared the bejeesus out of you with
That. You think I'm some post-traumatic nut.

Pharus

Nah man, it's . . . it's alright.

Cabbie

Bastard diplomats. You never know where or . . .
Who they are but I swear if I meet one, I'll mash his
face in
Steal his friends and fuck his wife.

Pharus (*to us*)

Ding ding ding.
Ever thought of modelling?

*Outside Move offices. The party has ended. Lord
Fairway and Aunt Marian laugh wickedly.*

Aunt Marian

Lord Fairway, did you enjoy the party?

Lord Fairway

Well, I do love a scandal.
Bad news about that Sylvia Watson.

Aunt Marian

Yes, I wonder how Val will handle all of it.

Lord Fairway

You're not stepping in?

Aunt Marian

Would you rather?

Lord Fairway

Oh no, I'm afraid you've made a mess already with
this modelling thing. I mean, where's your man? I'm
starting to doubt your ability to make good decisions
for the company. You don't even have the first talent
signed.

Pharus enters.

Pharus
I actually signed two, maybe three on the way.

Aunt Marian
My goodness, my, my goodness.
I didn't know it would be like seeing
A ghost. You're Charlie's boy sure as day!
My sister's face in there, I see it like . . .

Pharus
Aunt Marian, don't cry.

Aunt Marian
Just dust and memories, dust and memories.
But enough of that. I'm your boss now,
Your Great Aunt Marian no longer.

Lord Fairway
Ahem.

Aunt Marian
Sorry, dear. Pharus, this is one of our . . . oldest board
members, Lord Fairway.

Lord Fairway
Marian!

Aunt Marian
Oh, my mean friend, what would we do if not tease
and truth?
I'm afraid you've missed the party, you arsehole,
It was great fun even if impromptu. What took you?

Pharus
On the way I signed up some models, or at
Least prospectives.
But they may
Need us to sponsor them for work visas –

Aunt Marian
That's nice, dear.

Pharus

Don't you want to hear?

Aunt Marian

I believe you, I do. But I realised that I left my
American friend and he gets nasty if he's
Over-cooled. Need to grab him before
I go off to bed. You can fill me in on it all later.
I expect you here ten sharp on Monday. Want to see
all you've got!
DON'T BE LATE!

Aunt Marian exits.

Pharus

Night. I didn't know there were so many Americans
here.

Lord Fairway

Oh, this one has been around for ages.
Her old friend Jack –

Pharus

– Nicholson?

Lord Fairway

Daniels.

Pharus

I see.

Lord Fairway

We all have our vices. For instance
I like to watch . . . and listen.

Pharus

Huh.

Lord Fairway

Tell me about these new prospectives.
Are they as talented as you?

73

Pharus

You are too kind, My Lord.

Lord Fairway

Ooh, I do like the way you say that.

Pharus

Been practising.
Lets not be bashful, My Lord, we see
Each other. A man of your stature,
Is there an odd angle I can help you reach?

Lord Fairway

I should be appalled at whatever you are
Suggesting. I don't even know what you are speaking
Of but I sense it's dirty, underhanded and plain illegal.

Pharus

So you don't?

Lord Fairway

Oh, but I do. And it's just . . . my wife . . .
Well I have, perhaps you
Being such a well travelled man have heard . . . My
friends
Talk about this new marriage therapy. I've not tried it
But you could be just the man to help. See, we would
have you and maybe your roughest international
representative over
For a light dinner, and . . . we'd then discourse some
personal
Intimate marital problems.

Pharus

Specifically dealing with . . .

Lord Fairway

Her satisfaction.

Pharus

I see.

Lord Fairway
Of course you see! All you –

Pharus
Blacks.

Lord Fairway
Quite.
Have some advantage to understanding
The feral physical nature of women –
I fear I'm being offensive.

Pharus
No fear.

Lord Fairway
My only satisfaction is in seeing her sated.
Being satisfied. I hate to burden you on your
First day.

Pharus
What are we here for if not to help?

Lord Fairway
Of course we won't need to speak of our . . . discourse,
With Auntie Marian or Cousin Val. Discretion –

Pharus
It's my middle name.

Valentina enters.

Lord Fairway
Oh hello, Valentina!
This is . . . Have you met your cousin, Pharus?
He's a lovely man you could learn so much from
Him. I'll call you about . . .

Pharus
This weekend, My Lord, absolute pleasure to help.

Lord Fairway
Great. Ta!

Lord Fairway exits. Val and Pharus size each other up.
We hear western-movie music, they square off and
draw, Clint Eastwood-style.

Pharus
This doesn't have to be awkward.

Valentina
But it is.
What took you so long?

Pharus
Who's Sylvia?

Valentina
Nothing, I mean something, but she's fine,
And I can handle it so stop asking, and it's none
Of your business, you can't have my job!

Pharus
I . . . Huh . . . I'm here . . .

Valentina
You can't do my job. You don't know my job.
It's hard.

Pharus
You clean up after clients.

Valentina
I offer people a way to live publicly decently.

Pharus
Wow, wow, cousin, she painted you wrong.
Auntie made you seem like you were, you know,
Kind of naive or delusional. But it's much, much worse.
You're actually really sweet *and* you've got integrity.

Valentina

And from what I've learned in the past eight hours
About you, sir, is that you aren't and . . . do not.
What kind of man up and takes a job in a completely
contrary field just
Because his aunt offered?

Pharus

Huh, in these recessionary times
I would say every man looking to prove himself.

Valentina

Oh don't give me that American bootstraps,
Bootstraps.
I've had enough 'Yes we can' to know when I'm being
Set up. And if it isn't for my job I've just got to figure
out
What.

Pharus

Well, how will you, cousin?

Valentina

Stop calling me that! Now, if you could please . . .
I need to finish up . . .

Pharus

I'm pretty tired anyway from all that working. Car
coming up, is that for you?

Valentina

Yes, nosey, if you don't mind . . .

Pharus

Night.

Pharus exits. Red enters.

Valentina

Did any press see who was in the car?

Red

No, but some nutter tried to get in my car before
They arrived, said he worked here. Security grabbed him.
Thank God I called back and found out that
Their flight was delayed.

Valentina

Good, very good,
Let me speak to him briefly, but you can
Take them to their hotel right after. Hey?

Red

Yes.

Valentina

Thank you.

Red

I didn't think you would say anything.

Valentina

You know I appreciate you.

Red

Thank you.

Valentina

You've been so good to me.

Red

I know.

Valentina

It won't be long.

Red

I've heard that before, Valentina.

Red exits. Jules walks up with Loni in tow.

Valentina

Jules Mac Mana!

Jules

You must be
Valentina?

Valentina

How was your trip?
So glad you could make it.

Jules

Glad you could see us.

Valentina

We are more than thrilled that you've accepted my
invitation
For us . . . to handle your PR . . . situation. Welcome
to the UK, Jules.

Jules

Thank you, Valentina.

Valentina

It's just Val.

Jules and Loni exit.

Just Val.

Act Four

Bedroom of Lord Fairway.

Lord Fairway
A word.

Pharus
I'm so sorry, My Lord . . .

Lord Fairway
Please don't interrupt me.

Pharus
Sir.

Lord Fairway
I brought you here, Pharus, because
I thought you trustworthy. I thought you
Discreet . . .

Pharus
You have my sincere –

Lord Fairway
Let me finish, you little fuck, I do not like
Being disrespected in my own house. You hear?

Pharus
Absolutely, sir.

Lord Fairway
Now I wanted your home boy to satisfy my wife but
I intend to put my hands anywhere I see fit
And if your man has a problem with it then he
Should keep his cock to himself.

Pharus

Ragiv's new, he didn't know . . .

Lord Fairway

What's not to know? I pay you for sex.
I picked you because you were family to
Marian. You think I haven't been through this
Before with some lunk-head coming through here
Trying to extort money or threaten violence?

Pharus

What can I do to make this right, Lord Fairway?

Lord Fairway

I don't ever want to see that little shit again.

Pharus

Done. You don't have to see either us again, sir.

Lord Fairway

Why would that be? That would be quite a shame.

Pharus

My Lord?

Lord Fairway

I mean I thought I was a keeper of the flame?
Your Aunt Marian doesn't know this is what
You are really doing, yes? We wouldn't want her
Catching on.

Hands him a cheque.

Don't worry, Pharus, I'll
Keep these little ducats coming – and I also have a
friend.
I told him all about you.
You see, I'm already helping you spread your business.
We have to keep in contact. I can keep my hand on you.
I would hate to have to come to 'Move' looking
For you. Whenever I'm there, I have a tendency to talk
too much.

Presentation room at Move.

Valentina
You sound wonderful! You're not too weak – you are up for this?

Sylvia
I am.

Valentina
Good, good. I don't want you to feel rushed.

Sylvia
I'm rushing myself. Can't believe I . . .

Valentina
It's in the past.

Sylvia
It's in the *Guardian*.

Valentina
True, true, and that . . . that's my fault, I underestimated the apathy
And cynicism of the media by announcing . . . my bad. Ha! But now
We're trying to show life, and that's noble.

Sylvia
Is it?

Valentina
Of course, of course. We're on the right path.

Sylvia
Thanks.

Valentina
But that path has to be fast-tracked, I'm afraid.

Sylvia
Pardon?

Valentina

I . . . Listen, sister, the best way to make this all – the interview, the overdose – the best way to
Make it all go away is to make more news, better news.

She takes Sylvia's jumper.

Sylvia

What . . . what are you doing?

Valentina

When Jules gets here I need you to seduce him.

Sylvia

You want me to try and sleep with the CEO of Ditch Diggin' Records so he will give me a record deal?

Valentina

No, no, no. See? Good God, I believe in you. You are talented – he should give you a record
Deal based on your ability, your talent, your singing.
I want you to seduce him so he wants to date you.

Sylvia

Oh, is that all?

Valentina

Look, while you were gone some pretty amazingly stupid things happened. But if I can somehow parley your crisis into a triumph then I will, like the great Caesar Augustus, secure the realm for myself and make sure that you are well protected in the future, dear Cleopatra!

Sylvia

What? I don't understand.

Valentina

Understand this. Get him to date you or get dropped from the books.

Sylvia

Oh my God. I can't believe you said that.

Valentina

    This is how the game is played.
    This is how it's won. Don't do anything to
    Disrespect yourself. Don't lose anything
    You haven't lost, but if you want to stay in this
    If you really want a good chance at it,
    Listen to me. Show Jules you can sing and
    Then show him you can dance. It will
    Wash away a great deal of what's come before.

Sylvia

    I don't seem to have a choice.

Valentina

    We all have a choice. You've made some pretty
    harmful ones. Time to try again.

Back at the office.

Ragiv

    I said I was sorry!

Pharus

    What are you even doing here?

Ragiv

    Trying to make amends, you know.

Pharus

    Why? What for? I helped you out
    And you fucked me over.

Ragiv

    Well, technically –

Pharus

    I don't want your smart lip, man.

Ragiv

    Listen, I was out of my element, Pharus.
    Look at me. Do I look like a man who was

In full possession? He tried to grab my balls
While I fucked his wife, I panicked.
Tell me your first time out you didn't make mistakes?

Pharus

That was different.

Ragiv

Why?

Pharus

I was fifteen.

Ragiv

Fucking hell, you are a professional.

Pharus

I don't do business with fighters.

Ragiv

Me? I'm not. I don't have a fighting bone
In my body. I'm all romance and poetry.

Pharus

You can't get angry, you can't get jealous, or even
Excited. The key is to stay calm, stay calculating,
On your toes.
Feelings are dangerous, they can't be trusted.

Ragiv

Man . . . so much to learn. Will do, for next time we
head over.

Pharus

There won't be a next time there. They've asked
You not come back.

Ragiv

Those fuckers! *Just* because I wouldn't let that
Mary grab my Joseph, he wants to cancel us.

Pharus

Listen, like I said, you need to control yourself.

Qwik enters.

Qwik
Is fifteen minutes good, Pharus?

Pharus
Yeah!

Qwik exits.

Fuck, yeah.

Ragiv
Fifteen for what?

Pharus
You're a model, remember! Dammit, man. Am I the
only one that came to work today?

Ragiv
Cool it, Versace! I have a favour.

Pharus
Later –

Ragiv
Well, I brought someone I thought could help us out.

Pharus
What? What? Why?
I've got the showing for my aunt and cousin right now.
Ragiv, man, this ain't show-and-tell! Why you
Bringing friends to my, *faux*, place of work?

Ragiv
He's a refugee from Port au Prince. He's got
Nowhere to go, he's trying to get asylum,
But you know how long that could take.
I just thought we could . . .

Pharus
Fine. Let me see him. Man!

Ragiv

Be right back.

Ragiv exits. Officer Jeff Thibodeux enters with Svetlana.

Officer Jeff Thibodeux

Hiya, Pharus,

Pharus

Uh!

Officer Jeff Thibodeux

Just the man I wanted to see.
Svetlana, this is Pharus.

Svetlana

Hi. You make princess?

Officer Jeff Thibodeux

She doesn't speak much . . . Listen.
I can't stay long, just wanted to make sure beforehand
that
Her contract was in order.

Pharus

What? (*Sigh.*)
Listen. Officer Jeff, I'm not signing
A contract with Svetlana, alright? What's going
To happen is I'm going to show her today
To my boss and if she likes her we might send
Her off on a few jobs. And if she books them,
Then we can talk about signing exclusivity contracts,
Okay?

Officer Jeff Thibodeux

Wait, so she has to walk today?
Oh goodness, we gotta prepare.

Pharus

Well no . . . you . . . can't come.

Officer Jeff Thibodeux
Why not? I want to be right there to see it go on and if I
Suspect you are up to something for one second,
I will hand you over with more trumped-up
Charges than Interpol can handle.
I'll make it so you end up
Somewhere like Djibouti where they aren't
So kind to fair-skinned homosexuals.

Pharus
You're right. I'm sorry, Officer Jeff, you are right!
Please just
Wait for us in the presentation room and we will be
there in a moment.
I just want to . . . introduce Svetlana to the other
models.

Officer Jeff Thibodeux exits. Benton and Ragiv enter.

Benton
Hello?

Pharus
What in the Mandela is this?

Ragiv
My friend Benton.

Pharus
Your old friend Benton. Who's going to believe I hired
him as a model,
And who'd want him as a –

Benton
There was already a nice lady in the hallway
Offering to play a game of catch!

Cabbie (*entering*)
Hi!

Pharus
What happened?

Cabbie
Best ride of my life.

Pharus
Lord, it looks like the League of Nations up in here.
I guess a round of introductions is in order.
This is Svetlana who we will call, um, Slenda, that's
Cabbie, Ragiv who for some
Reason has brought his granddad, Toussaint L'Overtrue.

Benton
Why does he keep calling me old?

Pharus
Because ancient has more syllables.

Ragiv
Eh, lay off my man, Benton. He's cool.

Pharus
Do you have any idea what the job is here?

Everyone (*except Pharus*)
YES!

Pharus
You . . . you all do?

Svetlana
Absolutely, you've created cover of model agency
So we can continue to work as hooker.

Pharus
'Continue . . . created' . . . You speak English?

Svetlana
Of course I do. I've lived here nearly entire life.

Pharus
But what the hell did Border Patrol . . . Officer Jeff –

Svetlana
He's just lunk-head I trick into being trick.

Pharus

You . . . all this time . . . So you know what's going on?

Svetlana

The way you are running things, everyone will.

Pharus

That's why I usually work alone.

Cabbie

But we're glad you took us on.

Pharus

So you don't mind?

Cabbie

I love it!

Ragiv

Whoa, why are you so excited?

Cabbie

I went to pick up that lady you told me to . . . And at first I thought, well this is odd, why would he want me to pick her up, she seems fine arranging a ride for herself. Then she started talking to me about her diplomat husband and I just . . .

Pharus

You what?

Cabbie

It was bonkers . . . I mean I know myself to have a temper but there I was in this posh woman's face, breathing down her neck, smelling her expensive pearls and lace and . . . and she's there holding my face. I tell her how much I hate the cunt of a husband. And she pulls tight, really tight and kisses my face. Never felt anything like it. Like she was thirsty for me. My own wife never kissed me like that. Right there in the back of that cab, she pulls my hand under her skirt and the tightest wetness all over my fingers. I could

barely breathe I was moving so fast. I had to . . . I had
to have it.

Pharus
Did you?

Cabbie
Yes. She said that this was for you.

Pharus
Well just fifteen per cent is for Move.

Ragiv
Fifteen per cent?

Pharus
That's what any agency would take off new
Clients, trust me. Besides it's not the money that's
Of any real profit.

Benton
What's that?

Pharus
Cabbie, you gonna see your Snooty Lady again?

Cabbie
Well, she wants . . . Says she needs a driver when
She heads to Rome next week.

Pharus
Welcome aboard, Captain Cabbie, you're a kept man.
This is the thing you long and truly work for.
Don't let me have to tell you this again. You are
Not in the business for quantity, it's the quality.
If you are lucky or smart you have to find your *one*.

Benton
Like Frodo?

Ragiv
Like Neo!

Svetlana

Like Bono.

Pharus

It's lucky for Cabbie to have found his
So soon. In the meantime till you've located your
Benefactor you can't have great expectations.
We should talk about some 101s. You let
Me know if I'm going too fast, Papa Smurf.

Benton

You just try to keep up with me.

Pharus

You got your blue pills, Morpheus?

Benton

What? My heart pills?

Pharus

Your dick pills.

Benton

I don't need no pills.

Pharus

The art if there is any, is in the dick.
The profession is harder on women but
The art is a bitch for men.

Ragiv

Because?

Svetlana

Woman can fake turned on. Some women do that and
they not
Even prostitute. Man: one false move and dick goes
down.
Dick's hard: someone farts, dick goes down. You walk
into hotel,
Smells like dried fermented and sulphuric

Vomit marinated with two butts
And half a fuck, then find Jabba the hut type
Individual wheezing on machine, playing with
Small monkey's finger and bastard keep asking you
Repeatedly 'I'm sexy, right?' Takes master to say yes
to this and
Stay hard. And that's what you are paid for.

Pharus

Where the fuck did you come from?

Svetlana

East London.

Pharus

Listen, with all due respect, I'm not comfortable with
you . . . You know, trading a trick. I haven't worked a
woman. But maybe you can help me run ground
operations from home.

Svetlana

You won't let me trade trick but you'll let me be
secretary?

Pharus

No! Well, yes. Please.

Svetlana

Where do I sit?

Pharus

I'll show you now.

Qwik enters.

Qwik

I just came to tell you that Val and Marian are set.
They want to start the viewing.

Pharus

Great. Uh, models, walk.

Svetlana and Qwik trail.

Qwik
You're a model?

Svetlana
You a man?

Qwik
Ooh, she scares me!

Another part of Move.

Jules
Man, you can sing!
But we gotta find you some new material . . .

Sylvia
What do you think of this sweater?

Jules
Um, yeah it's nice.

Sylvia
The Jules Mac Mana. Been listening to your jams since
primary, innit.

Jules
When?

Sylvia
Forever. It's true, you know Rick Ross, and P Diddy,
And them?

Jules
Yeah, I, ha, rolled with them fools.

Sylvia
Mm, wicked!

Jules
Nah, they ain't as bad as they seem.

Sylvia

What about you? You a good guy or a bad boy?

Jules

I'm a . . . I'm a man.

Sylvia

I bet you got a crazy side to you. I mean, you're
A businessman, anyone can see that, but what
Else? You got an inner freak?

Jules

Apparently you do.

Sylvia

That's what I'm saying, that's what I need.
Someone who helps me bring out that inner
Exotic. For some reason since you came in, I been
Feeling different.

Jules

Look, I was saying . . .

Sylvia

Sick of being sad. Wanna sing soul and sultry.
Wanna get down but I need somebody to help me
Find that. Can you do that, Jules? Can you be my
Muse and my manager?

Jules

Whoa, girl. What you . . . you trying to
Do?

She straddles him.

Sylvia

To play the game, Jules. I need you to
Sign me up.

She produces a pen and her chest.

Jules

Listen –

Sylvia

Sign me to Ditch Diggin' Records.
I could be your female protégé. Learning everything
I need to know from you. You can mould me, teach me.
I can emerge The Lady Syl of Soul. But I need someone
To help me dig deep.

Jules

Whoa, ha, slow down.

Sylvia

Can't, Daddy, I choose fast –

They kiss.

Model showing.

Pharus

It isn't often that a man is called upon to take a little
time and space
And create, where perfection lay before, new, better.
Where would I go to find the fresh spring water to
compete with the salt of the earth?
I decided to dig deep into the well, the ground, on
which I was standing and begin to understand, to take
in, the bustling cosmopolitan sprawl that is London.
Using my keen eye for talent, I sought to challenge the
fashion industry's bland template for waif and pale
and bring it an array that displays the true world
village that we've thatched under this grey northern
sky. Mr Qwik, dim the lights.

Qwik

Lights!

Pharus

Aunt Marian, Cousin Val, Officer Jeff, I offer you –
Models at Move.

The models come out in the order that Pharus
announces them. They are all dressed up in some
weird chic depending on what he says. The showing
becomes more a circus with Pharus the carnival
barker.

First up, we have Ragiv, stripped out of the streets of
London. Ragiv represents a longstanding tie that
London has with the Asian world. His lithe exterior
with his rough good looks allow him to easily glide
from gentleman, businessman, in a flash, to street bad
boy perfect for all the pay as you go SIM card
companies itching to get a niche. Thank you, Ragiv.

Valentina

That's a model?

Aunt Marian

Shhh!

Pharus

Next up we have Cab . . . I mean Callow. Yes, Jacob
Callow, he represents the often misunderstood
working-class hero. His nice smile and his shy ways
make him a new but familiar face. You'd love to enjoy
a pint with this regular lad, just don't mention the
credibility of Britain's diplomats.

Cabbie goes postal, crazy, series of 'Fuck you's.

He instantly becomes the face of protest, the voice of
the assembly. His verve to fight the power as it were
will be a great asset to campaigns for the Green Party,
Oxfam and OutRage. Thank you, Jacob.
And here . . .

Officer Jeff claps loudly.

Is clearly a company favourite. Slenda comes all the
way from the mythic land of Prussia. And with her tall

stature and striking poses, she'd surely become a runway favourite. If she could walk in heels. But forget the heels –

She kicks them off.

This girl's got spunk, she's got pizzazz, she can . . . crawl on all fours and growl like . . . like a lion? Where the . . . Thank you, Slenda!

Valentina
But she's *too* tall.

Officer Jeff Thibodeux
And you're too butch.

Pharus
Ladies and gentlemen, please . . .
There is one other model A bit of a dark horse. A bit of an old horse.
Benton! I've decided to try and break into a more commercial appeal with this Haitian immigrant. Every placard advertisement for diversity needs a poster child.
And Benton . . . is . . . that. With his cool swagger and ginormous, gravity-defying,
Head. It's amazing he's remained upright all these years and he also
Sings – no, dances, and does . . . that thing too. Yeah, let's give a round of applause for our models.

Valentina
Un-be-lievable!

Aunt Marian
I'll say!

Valentina
You expect us to believe this cast of village idiots is our roster?

Aunt Marian
I love it.

Valentina
You what?

Qwik
She loves it.

Valentina (*to Qwik*)
Move!

Aunt Marian
I knew I could count on you, Pharus.

Valentina
Mother, these models –

Aunt Marian
Are perfect.

Valentina
– will bring about our ruin, I can't believe . . .
Half of them aren't even the proper size.
One of them looks like he might need assisted living.

Aunt Marian
Well done, Pharus. Care to grab a celebratory drink?

Pharus
Oh . . . oh no, thank you, Aunt Marian, I'm still on
The clock.

Aunt Marian
Suit yourself.

Valentina
Mother . . .

Valentina, Aunt Marian and Qwik exit.

Officer Jeff Thibodeux
Wonderful, see you at home?
Princess?

Slenda giggles. Officer Jeff exits.

All
We did it!

All exit.

Corridor at Move.

Valentina
Mother!

Aunt Marian
Uh-oh, she's mad now.

Valentina
I want you to retire.

Aunt Marian
You do something worth my resignation
And I will.

Valentina
No! Listen to me! You need to step down
And hand control of Move to me right now.
All my life I have worked so hard and now
It's becoming a nightmare because you decided
To bring some gigolo over from the States to
Run your modelling agency.

Aunt Marian
So you found out?

Valentina
Found out?

Aunt Marian
But you know he's a . . .

Valentina
Cocky little shit?

Aunt Marian

Lord, you people are slow. Lord Fairway called me,
trying to gloat. Poor bastard could never keep a secret,
thought he had finally one-upped me. 'Oh, hello,
Marian, how are you? I had an adorable meeting with
Pharus. Lovely boy. Lovely.' Right then I decided to
burst his bubble. I said, 'Poof the Magic Dragon, I
know Pharus is a hustler and by now
Has probably popped your top. I also know that as we
speak
He is currently recruiting others under the guise of
models for the company.'

Valentina

I . . . I . . . I . . . How?

Aunt Marian

I background-checked him before he came over.

Valentina

He has a record?

Aunt Marian

No, he's too smart for that. But he has many friends
and they are all powerful
Older people who he's 'assisted' for. All that took was
a phone call.

Valentina

And you still hired him! You've got to get rid of him!

Aunt Marian

You just told me to step down. Next, you are going to
say that you didn't know it was me who set up Sylvia
for that awful run-in with the pap.

Valentina

Mother, how could you?

Aunt Marian

I was trying to wake you up.

Valentina

Jesus, mother, if Pharus . . . ?
Are they . . . ? My God!

Aunt Marian

It gets better. Wait till the rest of it comes out.

Valentina

There's more! How are you so willingly-nillingly
Going towards annihilation?

Aunt Marian

Easily, I'm ready to go. I have been.
This all blows up, I have enough offshore on-shore to
be great
Until my twilight. But
What will happen to you then, Val, when they find
Whores on the books and a pimp named Pharus
Fucking the board? Here is your chance, darling
Tina. Here's your chance. Go.

Another part of Move.

Loni

Yo, where's Val? Jules wants to see her?

Qwik

Can you tell me the purpose?

Loni

'Cause we here on business, because
He said he wanted to see her, because
You pissing me off answering my question
With a question. Where is Val?

*Loni moves into Qwik and lays hands on him. Pharus
enters with Ragiv.*

Pharus

Listen to me close. You can't expect to only

Get the kind of jobs you like. I'm sending you
Out to work, not have fun.

Loni

What the fuck, Pharus?

Pharus

What in the shit! Uh . . .

In a strong Scottish accent.

It's Fergus to you, mate.

Loni

Nah you . . . you Pharus.

Pharus

I get that all the time, that I look
Like some kith or kin of many a
Person but I'm definitely Fergus from
Up around Glasgow way. True's God
I'm wondering who you are?

Loni

I'm Loni. And I used to pound a kat named
Pharus, look just like you.

Pharus

I'm into the women.
Don't deal with the homos, sorry lad.
(*To Ragiv.*) Lets go!

Loni

No, I mean, beat him up. You sure you ain't him?

Pharus

You seem a bit thick, you do,
But I assure you I'm not him. I work
Here at Move, me and my associate . . .

Ragiv

Adul Kalam.

Pharus
Yes, my fast-thinking great Indian associate
Adul –

Ragiv
Of the Pakistani Kalams.

Pharus
Oh my stars! My apologies there, lad, all this time
I took
You for Indian!

Ragiv
It's quite alright, for a second I thought you were
American.

Pharus
Joking, that wry humour they have down in the
Pakistani border, so rich and pungent and
Punched in the stomach.
We all work here at Move together with Mr –

Qwik
Koler! From North of the Rhine.

Pharus
What!
I mean sure our –

Qwik
– German –

Pharus
– colleague.

Loni
Wait a second, a minute ago you sounded Brit?

Qwik
Yeah, I just do that for the Americans, so that
We can make ourselves seem more assimilated.
But this is the true nature of my speaking.

Loni

Something funny is going on here.

Pharus

Well, let's not have it go on for too long there, lad.
If you just tell me the nature of your visit.

Loni

Well, Jules Mac Mana my boss is getting represented
by Val and . . . Are you sure you ain't him?

Pharus

Lord for the Christ of might come down peace,
Rain down night! I am a cut from the tartan sure as
the day is long!

Loni

If you Scottish, why you so brown then!

Ragiv

Well, you've heard of Black Irish? He's Brown Scot.

Pharus

As brown as a Scotch egg and my mother wherever she
is would
Roll over if she heard you calling me anything else.

Ragiv

Yes.

Qwik

Ja!

Loni

I'm getting the hell out of here. Yo, Jules!

Loni exits.

Pharus

Thanks, Qwik. Le's go!

Pharus and Ragiv exit.

Qwik

I love that game.

Slenda enters.

Slenda

Mr Qwik!

Qwik

Ms Slenda!

Slenda

Here are the final documents to send to HR.
Please give me confirmation of when the process will
be complete.

Qwik

You're not my boss.

Slenda

I'm your boss's secretary.

Qwik

Well, that makes you my secretary. You do what I say.

Slenda

Listen to me, little shit, I will
Smash your face in and pour boiling tea through asshole.
You spout this
Shit to someone more inclined to hear.

Qwik

Slenda! I love you.
I never knew terror like I do with you.
Please tell me more, more pain.

Slenda

Oh, you are liking tha' hurt?

Qwik

Desperately.

Slenda
> Sit
> On floor . . .
> Crawl
> Into office.
> Go!

> *Qwik exits.*

> Just remember . . . first one's free, all others cost.

Outside Move.

Ragiv
> So wait, you used to trick for Jules Mac Mana?

Pharus
> No, it never got that far. I was grooming him
> To be my number one but he's fucking nuts.
> Was trying to tie me up, or down. Whatever,
> It doesn't matter. Because he's here. Ugh,
> Why is this happening?

Ragiv
> Whoa, didn't think I'd see you panic.
> We'll figure out a way around him.

Pharus
> That's the thing, I thought I did. I mean, he should pretty
> Much be in jail. He should be trying to recoup the sales
> Loss and dealing with defamation of character suits
> that the Gay Lesbians of America have lobbed against
> him. Help me!

Ragiv
> That was easy for you to say.

Pharus
> Yes, you, you owe me. I found you in

A situation quite like this and now I need
Your help. All of the money made so far is still
Being processed.
But you need to go and meet this man
That Fairway set up.

Ragiv

No, man, I'm not . . .

Pharus

Fuck your moral high ground, man.
I need your help. Please.

Ragiv

Why don't you go?

Pharus

They'll be looking for me, not you.
I'll try and warn everyone else.
But if you go now you can get in and
Get out without suspicion. Get him to pay you
In cash and get back and then . . .

Ragiv

And then . . .

Pharus

And then we can, uh, catch a train to Paris.
Or something.

Ragiv

We?

Pharus

Be nice, right? We could start up
Something there. Just me and you. Us.
Could be nice, man.

Ragiv

Nice. You being cool and calculated?

Pharus
Yeah. That's the plan.

Ragiv
Got it.

Pharus
Thank you. Thank you so much, Ragiv.

Ragiv
Meet me back at yours?

Pharus
Yes, unless I've checked out . . . but just leave me a
message.

Ragiv
Good, good. Thank you, Pharus. Thanks.

Pharus
Thank you. Later.

Act Five

Office at Move.

Jules
Nah, nah, nah.
What, is this some kind of game to you people?

Loni
This ain't no game. You think he playing!

Sylvia
Calm down, babe.

Loni
Babe?

Jules
Uh, yeah, it's a long story.
This is bad news, bad, bad news.
I mean, you sure it was him?

Loni
Yeah, I'm pretty sure.

Valentina
It must be him, how many Pharus can the world stand?

Jules
Do you know what this kid did?

Sylvia
Did he hurt you, baby?

Jules
Stop that.
He left me in ruins all because I asked

Him to . . . to do me a favour. This punk set
Me up and I'm still digging out of the hate
Mail. Wait a minute, did you bring us over here to
humiliate us?
Oh, you in league with your lying-ass cousin?

Loni

I ain't scared to fuck-up a girl.

Valentina

Sit!
Oddly and sadly, I didn't know anything
About Pharus being in the mix with you
Two clowns. Dammit!
How is it these good intentions keep going
Oh-so-wrong? But they won't for long. Syl?

Sylvia

It's Lady Syl.

Valentina

Lady Syl, you think you could have some songs
Ready for tonight?

Sylvia

Yeah?

Jules

How can you be thinking about music at a time like
this?

Valentina

I had a few drinks before I came in.
Meaning we're going to start doing things
A li'l erratically round here. Jules, kneel down.

Jules

What?

Loni

Jules, what's going on?

Valentina
Lady Syl, approach him . . .

Loni
I think she's trynah knight you.

Valentina (*clicks a photo with her phone*)
I've had the most brilliant idea.
Tonight we're going to throw you a huge launch party!
Celebrating the retiring of Sylvia Watson and the birth
Of Lady Syl signed to Ditch Diggin' Records.

Jules
Now wait, we were still –

Valentina
Discussing how a male prostitute somehow infiltrated
The lives of one Jules Mac Mana, and one of the most powerful
PR firms, and managed to basically bring them shame, ruin, and
Scandal? No, I don't think we were discussing anything, Jules.

Jules
But what about Pharus?

Valentina
Let me worry about Pharus, he's family now.
Out! See you tonight. Go! Qwik!

Sylvia, Loni and Jules exit. Qwik enters, beat down.

Qwik
You called?

Valentina
Where have you been? Where are your clothes? And
why are you walking like that?

Qwik
I'm in love.

Valentina

Are you?

Qwik

Aw yes . . . yes, I am. I just love how she leans
Over me with that Prussian accent.

Valentina

Prussia doesn't exist . . . You mean Slenda!
Please, please, someone assassinate me.
Qwik, I need you to call the press for
Tonight; get every v-log, inside-track star,
Sun moon reporter, interested. I know it's
Short notice but tell them Lady Syl's got a secret.
You can't tell a soul, that on her near death
Bed a kind hip-hop mogul came to her aid and
Basically worked her back to health. Do not . . .
And whatever you do, do not send them the photo
That I've just sent to you on your phone.
I need you to hold it for safe-keeping.

Qwik

Safe with me.

Valentina

Also I need you to book a flight, to a small
Island like Martinique with a clime
More suited for elderly faculties.

Qwik

Are you . . .

Valentina

Do it now, Qwik. If you need me I'll be in my office
penning a letter.
NOW!

*Qwik exits followed by Valentina. Benton and Aunt
Marian come from behind a wall scantily clad. They've
just been having sex.*

Benton

So you knew I wasn't a real model? You knew this all the time?

Aunt Marian

Well, you didn't tell me, but I had an idea.

Benton

So where do we go from here?

Aunt Marian

I'm pretty sure that young lady there also
Known as my daughter will
Be freezing all my accounts but
I've got some cash stored under a light
Fixture in the women's loo.

Benton

Aw, please, you're my benefactor now.
No need to pay me with cash.

Aunt Marian

Oh, Benton, you are so romantic.

Benton

Race you to the loo.

Aunt Marian

Skip, skip, skip to my loo, my darling!

Outside a hotel in Mayfair. Pharus enters holding some cool small luggage and wearing dark shades. Girl Wonder enters dressed as a hotel desk attendant.

Girl Wonder

Sir, sir . . . Hi, hiya.
Are you checking out today?

Pharus

No, what makes you think that?

Girl Wonder

Well, the bags in hand and the incognegro expression
on your hater-blockers.

Pharus

My God, do you work everywhere?

Girl Wonder

No, just at the front desk, and chasing behind potential
bill-dodgers is outside my jurisdiction. (*Sotto voce.*)
Dick.

Pharus

Well, don't worry, all of the transactions for the stay
are on my card.

Girl Wonder

Your card has been declined.

Pharus

Well, I'm sure I have another . . .

Girl Wonder

No need to explain, a young man came
By and paid everything in cash.

Pharus

He . . . what?

Girl Wonder

Yes, sir. He did. And if he didn't, seems
Like we might not have gotten paid at
All. But that's alright, love, no need thinking
Of the ifs-and-ands. What's done is done and
You're leaving, no?

Pharus

Did he say anything?

Girl Wonder

Who?

Pharus

The young man?

Girl Wonder

Oh . . . that's right, he left a note for you.
Here you are. There you go. Bye-bye.

She exits. Pharus reads.

Pharus

'Pharus, came by to meet you but couldn't find
You. Left money to help you out,
Mate. Find me. I'm going to look for you at Move.'
Fuck!

A red carpet event.

Sherman Kanderebitz

WHAT UP YO!
This is your man Sherman K coming
To you *live* from the exclusive launch
Party of Lady Syl of Soul.
Formerly Sylvia Watson who
Has enjoyed a rebound in fame thanks
To the surfacing of a photo of her alleged engagement.
Rumours have been swirling along with the picture
that she's found a beau who's been by her side the
entire time of her unfortunate accident and will appear
with her at this launch. So your man had to be here
right outside the launch party
In the flesh to see: WHAT UP YO!

Valentina

Sherman! As loud and in-your-face as always.

Sherman Kanderebitz

No doubt.

Press (*all*)
Val, Valentina, right here, Val.

Press 2
Val!

Valentina
Welcome. Thank all of you for coming.

Press 2
You look amazing.

Press 1
Who's your dress by?

Valentina
This old thing?
No, this evening isn't about me at all
But our lovely client Lady Syl. And
Move is proud to present her this evening.

Press 3
What about your mother?

Press 1
The legendary Marian of Move, is she satisfied
With the direction of Syl and the company?

Valentina
What you see here is the fruition, the flowering of
Her years of work, dedication, and training.
This is the same woman who for years made
Sure we answered the phones with a kind 'Hiya'
Instead of 'Hello'. She was that particular.

Press 1
Was?

Valentina
Earlier our dear Marian, my mother,
Admitted that she had lost her will for the company.

So based on her own words and
Suggestion, she decided to take a leave that will
Eventually grow into a retirement and take
On more of an advisory position.

Press 2
What of the rumour of Models at Move?

Press 1
Yeah, wasn't that your mother's idea?

Valentina
Huh. The modelling division at Move has been cleared and scrapped I'm afraid, so that we can focus on our very long and exclusive clientele. Thank you.

Sherman Kanderebitz
Val, sources say you threatened lawsuits and locks
In the loony bin if your mother didn't
Leave the company and say you sent her to a more
Carib place with a bottle of Irish and a fellow named
Benton.

Valentina
Sherman, I don't know where you get these ridiculous sources –

Sherman Kanderebitz
Uh, a fellow named Swift?

Valentina
Qwik!

Sherman Kanderebitz
'Sup?

Valentina
Fast, yes. But no, the leaving was all amicable. But it is true
As you said, my mother has met someone who in her golden years makes her happy.

I . . . I am only happy to announce that I may have
found the same.
This is my date. Red.

Red enters. She looks amazing.

Press (*all*)
Over here, Red! Red, over here!
Lovely dress, Red!
How long have you been dating?
Red . . . is it just Red?

Valentina
See you all inside!

Sherman Kanderebitz
There you have it, folks, confirmation of lesbian
activities!
And both of the chicks are hot! That's WHAT UP YO!
But back to the carpet – here comes the woman of the
hour,
Lady Syl.

Press (*all*)
Syl, right here! Syl!

Press 1
Syl, that is a sick suit.

Sylvia
It's Lady Syl, fellas.

Sherman Kanderebitz
What about the overdose, Lady Syl? Was that on
purpose or –?

Sylvia
You can't accidentally swallow that many pills. I knew,
Or thought I knew what I was doing, but I just needed
A place where I could come to express myself. Where I

Could get deeper than just some funny lines and magic
tricks.
I think you will see that in the music I'm making and
in the steps I'm taking.

Press 1
What are those?

Press 3
Was the proposal real?

Press 2
You really seeing a gangsta rapper who has been by
your side
All along? You still hate your fans?

Sylvia
We can't dwell on the past. Gotta look to the future.
That's what my friend says.

Press 1
Who's this friend?

Sylvia
Oh, he'll be along in a second. I thought you guys
might already know him.

Enter Jules and Loni. Jules holds Lady Syl's hand.

Press (*all*)
Jules!

Press 3
You're with Jules Mac Mana!

Sylvia
We're fast friends.

Press 1
How long have you been friends?

Press 2
Where do you see this going from here?

Press 1

Jules, are you the man in the photo?

Press 2

Jules, they say you don't like gays.

Sylvia

Not true.

Jules

Nah, our PR agent –

Press 2

– is a gay?

Jules

And I have nothing but love for her.

Sylvia

She's how we met.

Sherman Kanderebitz

Syl, what if he calls you a bitch like he does in his
record?
Hoes for mofos

(*Sings.*)
'*I need to make a switch
So I'm trading in the bitch.*'

Jules

What! You need to find some respect. Her name is
Lady Syl
And that's all I will be calling her. Check it!

Syl, Jules and Loni exit.

Sherman Kanderebitz

WHAT UP YO!
You seen it here first! The Lady and Lord
Of the Soul entering into what must be heaven.
But for now, this is your man Sherman K signing off!

The room shifts, closing out Sylvia and the crowd. It makes a space like a small office. Valentina enters and lights shift. Pharus is there.

Valentina

What on earth are you doing here? How'd you even get in?

Pharus

Qwik.

Valentina

Huh, well, escort yourself out please or I will call the –

Pharus

No, don't . . . don't do that. It's all me.
Listen, you can let the others go. I'm to blame.

Valentina

Blame for what?

Pharus

Come on, cousin . . . You know what I am saying. Just let him go.

Valentina

Who are you talking about?

Pharus

Ragiv . . .
What's going on?

Valentina

Well I don't want to talk too long, I'd like to get back out to the party.
But there is
No one to let go of considering there were
No charges wrought because *no crimes were committed here at Move under my watch.*
Not by me, you or any band of sordid characters with Funny names. Understood?

Pharus

Starting to . . . Ragiv said he came here.

Valentina

Oh, you mean that note? Oh no that was me.
Yeah, I had
Qwik take it over. Did it work? Did I actually fool you
into believing . . .
Oh, and you came! You showed up! How sweet!
And you were going to, good God, help your friends!
How . . . Look, you have integrity, cousin, shame.
Shame. No, your Ragiv never came here. And
As I spoke to your nasty little buddy Lord Fairway,
He never showed for his appointment through him
Either. He just disappeared into the air. Like you should
Have done.

Pharus

Well, I had to say goodbye to your mother.

Valentina

Oh, please, she was basically the rat that sold you out.
But this is boring. This is a party. We need more guests.
Jules?

Jules

How you doing, Pharus?

Pharus

Wha . . . Where you going, cousin?

Valentina

Back to my party, cousin.

Pharus

Take me . . . take me with you.

Valentina

No, I was thinking not. You see there wasn't a
Way to get you to pay for all the damage you caused

Emotional and palpable. But I figured there must be
something you could trade in.

Pharus
Wait, Val, let me say . . .

Valentina
GRAB!

Jules grabs Pharus.

Jules
Now just hold still.

Pharus
Oh God.

Valentina
CARESS!

Jules caresses Pharus's cheek.

Jules
You know what I wanna play, don't you?

Pharus
Val?

Valentina
LIGHTS!

Blackout.